Marketing Information Systems

Creating Competitive Advantage in the Information Age

Kimball P. Marshall
Jackson State University

With contributions by Roger A. Pick
University of Missouri, Kansas City

boyd & fraser publishing company
I(T)P   An International Thomson Publishing Company

Danvers • Albany • Bonn • Boston • Cincinnati • Detroit • Madrid • Melbourne
Mexico City • New York • Paris • San Francisco • Singapore • Tokyo • Toronto • Washington

DEDICATION

To Wilma Goetz of the University of St. Thomas in Houston, Texas, who taught me how to do research, and to Hardy Fuchs, who, as an administrator at Washington University in St. Louis, Missouri, kindly introduced me to the practical basics of database designs.

Executive Editor: James H. Edwards
Editorial Assistant: Stacey P. Emig
Production Editor: Barbara Worth
Manufacturing Coordinator: Lisa Flanagan

Marketing Director: William Lisowski
Interior Design and Composition: Gex, Inc.
Cover Design: Diana Coe

 © 1996 by boyd & fraser publishing company
A division of International Thomson Publishing Inc.

I(T)P   The ITP™ logo is a trademark under license.

Printed in the United States of America

This book is printed on recycled acid-free paper that meets Environmental Protection Agency standards.

For more information, contact boyd & fraser publishing company:

boyd & fraser publishing company
One Corporate Place • Ferncroft Village
Danvers, Massachusetts 01923, USA

International Thomson Publishing Europe
Berkshire House
168-173 High Holborn
London WCIV 7AA United Kingdom

Thomas Nelson Australia
102 Dodds Street
South Melbourne
Victoria 3205 Australia

Nelson Canada
1120 Birchmont Road
Scarborough, Ontario
Canada M1K 5G4

International Thomson Editores
Campos Eliseos 385, Piso 7
Colonia Polanco
11560 México D.F. México

International Thomson Publishing GmbH
Konigswinterer Strasse 418
53227 Bonn, Germany

International Thomson Publishing Asia
Block 211, Henderson Road #08-03
Henderson Industrial Park
Singapore 0315

International Thomson Publishing Japan
Hirakawa-cho Kyowa Building, 3F
2-2-1 Hirakawa-cho Chiyoda-ku
Tokyo 102 Japan

1 2 3 4 5 6 7 8 9 10 E 9 8 7 6 5
ISBN: 0-87709-290-7

Contents

PART 3   *DECISION SUPPORT SYSTEMS AND ARTIFICIAL INTELLIGENCE IN MARKETING*...53

Chapter 5   Decision Support Systems for Marketing...............................54

Chapter 6   Artificial Intelligence in Marketing 68

PART 4   *CREATING A MARKETING INFORMATION SYSTEM*..................81

Chapter 7   Planning a Marketing Information System 82

Preface

Nobody can say exactly when the first marketing information system was developed. Effective management of sales, products, pricing, advertising, and distribution in any business has always required that marketing managers organize the data available to them so they can use the data efficiently when they make decisions. As organizations and their information resources grew, so did their need for systematic approaches to managing marketing information. Recognizing this, Cox and Goode in 1967 published a pioneering article in the *Harvard Business Review* outlining the broad aspects of marketing information systems (MKIS) and the issues involved in developing these systems (see also Buzzell, Cox, and Brown, 1969). Since then, advances in computer-based information systems have created new tools and opportunities for marketing managers (Higby and Farah, 1991; Fletcher and Buttery, 1988). Well-designed information systems for marketing are now clearly recognized as sources of strategic competitive advantage.

The objective of this book is to provide an understanding of the basic components of marketing information systems and the fundamental processes by which these systems can be developed. As we will see, an effective marketing information system cannot be purchased "off the shelf." Although some components of a good system will draw on available commercial software and data, each organization must design its own system in light of its own objectives, information requirements, and approaches to decision making. In most cases, however, the key components of marketing information systems will be similar, and similar processes may be suggested for planning, developing, and implementing these systems.

Marketing Information Systems is organized into four parts. Part 1 introduces the concept of marketing information systems. Chapter 1 defines the term *marketing information system* (MKIS) and considers its special features. This chapter also identifies the basic components of this type of information system. Chapter 2 discusses how marketing information systems benefit organizations by providing competitive advantage through improved decision making.

Part 2 explores the wide range of data resources available to most organizations. Chapter 3 focuses on internal data resources by considering transaction processing data such as order entry systems, shipping systems, sales commission records, and accounts receivable systems. Sales transaction data is particularly important to marketing management because it allows managers to track product sales over time, assess the impact of promotional activities, identify possible problem areas, and so forth.

Chapter 4 addresses external data resources. First we will consider the opportunities and benefits of the exciting area of electronic data interchange (EDI) through communications among business partners' information systems. EDI allows marketers to monitor sales and inventories throughout the distribution channel and to establish automatic reordering systems that permit the organization to work closely with its customers to the benefit of all partners. Next we will review the world of third-party data resources, which have been made possible by the widespread use of automatic identification systems and public and private electronic data sources. These data resources include marketing environment data subscription services such as those available through the U.S. government, private data vendors, and on-line data services; single-source data services; and market research projects.

Part 3 of *Marketing Information Systems* introduces several types of software used to analyze marketing data. Chapter 5 begins this discussion by addressing the use of decision support systems in marketing. This chapter reviews how common sales and cost reporting and inquiry systems provide information to marketing managers and how information contained in such systems may be linked to other decision support tools to provide even greater utility. Decision support tools may range from analytical models to executive support systems. Chapter 6 extends the discussion of available software by addressing the intriguing area of artificial intelligence and opportunities for expert systems and neural networks in marketing.

The last section of *Marketing Information Systems*, Part 4, focuses on the creation of an effective marketing information system. Chapter 7 introduces a three-stage process for developing a MKIS—planning, technical development, and implementation—and provides a detailed discussion of the planning stage, including the steps of securing executive commitment, developing a MKIS team, carrying out a marketing audit, setting goals, developing macrospecifications, and budgeting. Chapter 8 addresses the technical development stage and considers eight steps: database design, hardware requirements, software requirements, communication requirements, systems controls, user interfaces, prototyping, and testing. Chapter 9 focuses on implementation procedures that will help ensure managers actually use the system, with emphasis on phased implementations of MKIS modules, user training, feedback, and system modifications. Chapter 10 concludes this book by considering how marketing information systems will develop in the future. The appendix is provided to introduce basic concepts of databases and their design to readers who may not yet be familiar with these topics.

In summary, *Marketing Information Systems* is designed to introduce you to the basic components of MKIS and how MKIS can contribute to competitive advantage. The book provides practical knowledge regarding resources that can improve marketing decision making and practical guidance for establishing a comprehensive, flexible information system to support marketing planning and management.

ACKNOWLEDGMENTS

Several people and organizations have made *Marketing Information Systems* possible and deserve my heartfelt thanks. Professor Roger A. Pick of the University of Missouri—Kansas City deserves a special thank-you. Dr. Pick encouraged me in the development of this book and generously served as a colleague with whom to exchange ideas. He contributed to the development of Chapters 3 through 6 and to the Appendix of this text.

Jim Edwards of boyd & fraser deserves special thanks for believing in the importance of this topic. Elizabeth S. MacDonell of Write One Consulting provided exceptional support as the developmental editor commissioned by boyd & fraser. Her patience and writing suggestions and her help in organizing this book and ensuring consistency across all chapters are sincerely appreciated.

The following reviewers also contributed valuable feedback:

Karen Becker	James Maskulka
Cedar Crest College	Lehigh University
Michael D'Amico	Paul Thistlethwaite
University of Akron	Western Illinois University
Joyce L. Grahn	Joanne Trotter
University of Minnesota–Duluth	Gwynedd-Mercy College
Roland Kushner	
Lafayette College	

Others deserve my thanks as well. Mr. Jimmy Carter of Mobile, Alabama, and Mr. John Gully of Austin, Texas, created the opportunities for me to gain the experiences needed to realize the importance of this topic to marketing practitioners and information systems managers alike. Professor Lyn Pankoff and Mr. Charlie Fuchs of the Simon School of Business at Washington University, St. Louis, Missouri, provided opportunities for me to personally experience the process of planning and implementing formal computer systems.

Finally, special thanks are given to colleagues in the International Business Schools Computing Association, the Midwest Marketing Association, and the American Marketing Association, all of whom provided professional forums in which these ideas could be explored. To my colleagues in these associations who provided feedback to me directly and who served as anonymous reviewers, thank you.

Introducing Marketing Information Systems

1

Fundamentals of Marketing Information Systems

Today more than ever, information is critical for effective business operations (Glazer, 1991). The wealth of information available to business managers grows exponentially each year, and the technologies available for processing this information are continually expanding. These changes make managing business information complicated and create opportunities for business managers who seek competitive advantage in the marketplace. In large part, these opportunities are direct results of the broader, ongoing revolution in information technologies. More than ever before, businesses are linked to global economies. Markets are quickly affected by competitors' actions, new government policies, changing technologies, shifts in consumer sentiment, and even changes in a company's own products, prices, salesforce, distribution systems, and promotional programs. To remain competitive in this information-dependent world, marketing managers must find new ways to manage information about changing market environments and the impacts of business decisions. Information must be managed in a way that provides guidance for decision making. This requires the planned development of marketing information systems.

WHAT ARE MARKETING INFORMATION SYSTEMS?

To understand what a marketing information system is and why it can be helpful to an organization, we must first understand what marketing is. The American Marketing Association (AMA) has defined **marketing** as "the process of executing the conception, pricing, promotion, and distribution of ideas, goods, and services to create exchanges that satisfy individual and organizational goals" (Bennett, 1988, p. 54). As we will see in the next chapter, the activities reflected in this definition cause marketers to be concerned with many aspects of the modern business organization, from planning and research and development to manufacturing, transportation, warehousing, and inventory control, as well as promotional programs and sales. To carry out these activities effectively, the marketing manager needs high-quality information and the tools to process it.

Reflecting the many types of marketing activities, the term *marketing information system* has been used by numerous writers to refer to a variety of computer applications, including sales lead systems, sales tracking and reporting systems, telemarketing systems, and customer support systems (Berenson, 1985; Dobrozdravic, 1989; Datapro Reports, 1989; Eisenhart, 1988; Moriarty and Swartz, 1989; Keon, 1987; Proctor, 1991). The term is sometimes also used to describe a computer-based approach to market research and intelligence (Churchill, 1991). As used in this book, the term **marketing information system (MKIS)** will refer to *a comprehensive and flexible, formal and ongoing system designed to provide an organized flow of relevant information to guide marketing decision making* (Marshall and LaMotte, 1992).

Our definition of a MKIS is designed to emphasize three key points. First, marketing information systems should be viewed as *comprehensive and flexible* because the marketing activities of a firm are interrelated and must adapt to changing environments. Sales results, for instance, are influenced by product availability, customer satisfaction, advertising, and so forth. Therefore, a well-designed marketing information system should be more than a sales lead system or a quarterly report of product performance; it should enable marketing managers to draw on diverse information as required by the marketing problem with which they are concerned.

Second, the system must be *formal and ongoing*. In other words, the system must be consciously designed with specific organizational goals in mind so that the system will meet the needs of marketing managers over an extended period. Marketing information systems are not just ad hoc, short-term systems developed by an individual manager to address a specific problem. Rather, they are deliberately developed to support ongoing marketing management decision making. To achieve this, specific organizational goals for the system must be established with knowledge about the jobs of marketing managers, and the development of the system must have broad organizational support and commitment.

Third, a marketing information system must provide an *organized flow of relevant information to guide marketing decision making*. The information must be relevant to marketing decision making. This means the system must be designed neither to provide all possible data nor to provide only data. Instead, the system must be designed to provide the types of data that will guide the company's decision making and provide the tools needed to transform this data into information that will help managers make wise, calculated marketing management decisions. To achieve this, the system must be designed to complement the decision-making processes of the organization while also meeting the needs and expectations of its users.

BASIC MKIS COMPONENTS

In its simplest form, a MKIS has five basic components. These are

- the internal environment;
- user interfaces;
- databases;
- applications software; and
- administrative supports.

A diagram of these is presented in Figure 1.1. As part of our introduction to the concept of a marketing information system, let us consider each of these components separately.

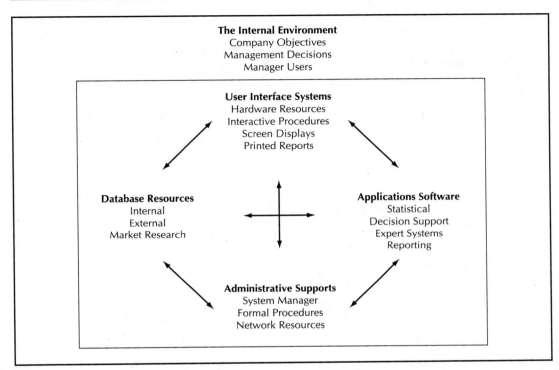

Note: Each of the five basic components of the MKIS are interrelated and influence one another within the context of the organization's internal environment. A comprehensive system perspective is needed for effective planning and development.

FIGURE 1.1   Basic MKIS Components

Internal Environment

A MKIS is designed to help marketing managers make decisions that effectively contribute to achieving company objectives. Therefore, the first component that must be considered in developing a MKIS is the internal environment. The **internal environment** includes

■   the managers who use the system;

■   the types of decisions they must make;

■   the corporate objectives that must guide decisions and the overall decision-making process; and

■   the cultural, social, and internal political factors that influence the organization's activities and decision making.

Questions that will help to define the types of data and analytical systems needed to support marketing management decisions include the following: How can a MKIS contribute to the company's objectives and therefore provide competitive advantage? What are the types of decisions marketing managers must make? What are the management questions that must be answered? What are the goals of the company? How do marketing managers in this company make decisions? Who must be involved in the decision processes? Who will be affected? In short, the company's objectives and marketing decision makers must be viewed as a basic component of a MKIS.

User Interfaces

The second basic component of a MKIS is the user interface. **User interfaces** are the processes and equipment by which the marketing manager will use the MKIS. These include

- the types of computers that users are willing to use;
- the way in which information is displayed on paper or on the screen of a terminal or microcomputer;
- the types of knowledge that may be required to use the system; and
- the printers and other forms of technology by which reports are produced to document the analysis underlying a decision.

The user interface system must be carefully designed with the needs and backgrounds of the managers in mind so that they will be willing to use the system as a helpful asset in their daily work.

Databases

Because good decision making requires the appropriate data, the third basic component of a MKIS is the database. A **database** is a well-organized collection of data files that can be used in conjunction with one another. Two categories of data are available to marketing managers: internal and external data. **Internal data** is information collected by the firm on a regular basis as a routine part of business activities, including internal movement of resources among departments and exchanges with the outside environment. Examples include sales records, shipping records, salesperson commission reports, and inventory information. **External data** is information provided by sources outside the company. Examples of external data include information provided by companies that specialize in monitoring market trends and sales, data provided by business partners with whom the organization exchanges information, and data provided by government agencies. Because data from many sources can affect marketing decision making and because the marketing manager may not be aware of all of the sources, designers of a MKIS must carefully study both the information that is now used and the types of additional information that might be helpful as well.

Data alone is not adequate. To be useful, data must be well organized. One of the most effective approaches to organizing data for the flexible needs of a marketing information system is as a systematic, well-documented relational database. A **relational database** is an organized set of data in which the various types of data items from several data sets are sufficiently identified by a predetermined set of criteria so that items may be linked together in a logical way.

For example, in a relational database, information on product sales might be recorded along with information on activities of individual salespeople. The record of a sale of a particular product (a *transaction*) would have information on the product, the price, the quantity sold, and the name of salesperson. The database record on the salesperson would include the salesperson's name as well as information on her or his sales quota, the office out of which he or she works, and the length of the person's employment with the company. In a relational database system, the salesperson's name (which appears on both the product sale record and the salesperson's record) could be used to relate the product sales records to the salesperson's records in order to create a new record. The new record would contain information from both the product and the salesperson records. With this type of combined record, managers could investigate whether more experienced salespeople sold more of a certain product, which sales offices sold more of a product, and similar questions that affect marketing decisions.

Clearly, a relational database system can be extremely useful for marketing decision making. Organizing extensive relational database systems can be a complex process that requires much planning; however, if the database system is well developed, maintained, and kept up to date, it can be the heart of a valuable MKIS.

Applications Software

Knowledge of how managers make decisions, the objectives of the company, and the database resources that are available will influence which types of decision support programs or systems are developed and maintained as part of the MKIS. **Applications software** is the fourth component of a MKIS. These are the programs that marketing managers use to access data in the database system and to analyze the data so as to provide information to guide marketing decisions. When used by a knowledgeable manager, applications software can transform the data in the database system into meaningful information that can give the company a competitive advantage in the marketplace.

Administrative Supports

Administrative supports provide the guidelines, processes, procedures, and personnel needed to maintain system integrity and to support managers using the system. If the MKIS system is to be an ongoing and effective support for marketing decision making, then there must be formal guidelines for processes and procedures governing the inclusion of data in the system and access to the data. There must also be clear definitions of the specific data items in the database and the market indicators that the applications software may produce. Administrative supports also include the system managers, who are responsible for maintaining the hardware and software, monitoring activities, and ensuring compliance with policies.

SUMMARY

In this chapter we have introduced a formal definition of a marketing information system (MKIS) and have reviewed its key components. As a comprehensive and flexible, formal and ongoing system designed to provide an organized flow of relevant information to guide marketing decision making, a MKIS can enhance the analytical capabilities of marketing managers. In this way, a MKIS can significantly improve tactical and strategic marketing decision making. But, as shown by the discussion of its components, a MKIS is also a complex type of information system. Careful planning will be required to design a successful system that is appropriate for a specific organization's internal environment. Also, substantial organizational resources will be needed to (1) identify, acquire, and organize the relevant data and applications software needed to support marketing decision making; (2) provide a user interface system that will be well received by the organization's marketing managers and staff; and (3) ensure the administrative supports that will be necessary for the MKIS to be maintained on an ongoing basis. While a clear understanding of the components of a MKIS and the MKIS development process can help to ensure success, it is also important that the organization's top-level managers and marketing managers understand how a MKIS can help achieve the organization's goals and establish competitive advantage in the marketplace. With the understanding of what a MKIS is and what its basic components are, let us now turn to Chapter 2 and consider how a MKIS can contribute to the organization's success and provide competitive advantage.

Key Terms

administrative supports
applications software
database
external data

internal data
internal environment
marketing

marketing information
  system (MKIS)
relational database
user interfaces

Berenson, C. (1985). "Marketing Information Systems." *Journal of Marketing*, Vol. 33 (October), pp. 16–23.

Cox, D. F., and R. E. Goode (1967). "How to Build a Marketing Information System." *Harvard Business Review*, Vol. 45, No. 3, pp. 145–154.

Kotler, P. (1991). *Marketing Management: Analysis, Planning, Implementation, and Control* (7th ed.). Englewood Cliffs, NJ: Prentice Hall.

Marshall, K. P., and S. W. Lamotte (1992). "Marketing Information Systems: A Marriage of Systems Analysis and Marketing Management." *Journal of Applied Business Research*, Vol. 8, No. 3 (Summer), pp. 61–73.

Proctor, R. A. (1991). "Marketing Information Systems." *Management Decision*, Vol. 29, No. 4, pp. 55–60.

2 *Marketing Information Systems and Competitive Advantage*

The information-intensive environment in which businesses operate today makes it critical that business managers have ready access to the information they require for good tactical and strategic decisions. This is especially true for marketing managers. The information required by marketing managers and the tools they use to analyze this information make up a complex system. This is because of the diversity of data and data sources on which marketing programs depend, the range of decision support tools required by marketing managers, and the variety of decisions involved in developing and carrying out marketing programs. Moreover, because marketing managers serve in a *boundary position*—sometimes called an interface—between the organization and its environments, the types of questions marketing managers ask and the types of information they need are often changing. For these reasons, we have chosen the definition of marketing information systems presented in Chapter 1—a definition that emphasizes flexibility. To review this definition, we said that a marketing information system is "*a comprehensive and flexible, formal and ongoing system designed to provide an organized flow of relevant information to guide marketing decision making*" (Marshall and LaMotte, 1992).

Perhaps the most important aspect of this definition is that a marketing information system provides information "to guide marketing decision making." Information systems that improve marketing decision making can provide a sustainable competitive advantage for the organization. A **sustainable competitive advantage** is an ability or resource that allows the organization to provide an offer to the market that is more acceptable to potential customers than competitors' offers and to maintain this preferred position over a long period. A MKIS can help to provide sustainable competitive advantage by improving marketing decision making as marketing programs are planned, implemented, and maintained over time. Further, a MKIS can improve marketing decision making by providing the appropriate data in a timely manner and by providing effective tools for analyzing relevant marketing data to produce information that can lead to effective decisions for achieving the organization's goals through marketing activities.

If we are to develop a MKIS that will be relevant to marketing decision making, we must first clearly understand what marketing managers do and the types of information that can help marketing managers make better and more timely decisions. In this chapter we will review how marketing can contribute to creating competitive advantage for the organization. We will then consider how marketing managers can use information about the firm's internal activities and external environments to create competitive advantage and achieve the organization's market objectives. Our own goal is to provide you with a clear understanding of the potential benefits a MKIS can offer. With this background, you will be better able to consider the more technical discussions of specific types of data sources presented in Part 2 of this book and the discussions of tools for data analysis and decision support presented in Part 3.

In popular usage the term *marketing* is often misunderstood. Some people use "marketing" to mean simply advertising and promoting products. Other people use "marketing" as a synonym for sales and selling. Sales activities, advertising, and promotions are all a part of marketing, but marketing has a much broader and deeper meaning than these terms suggest. In fact, the marketing department may be thought of as the **boundary department** that links the organization to its environment in order to create opportunities for exchange. As noted in Chapter 1, creating exchange opportunities involves many activities implied by the American Marketing Association's (AMA's) definition of **marketing** as "the process of executing the conception, pricing, promotion, and distribution of ideas, goods, and services to create exchanges that satisfy individual and organizational goals" (Bennett, 1988, p. 54).

Exchanges take place between the organization and its customers in the marketplace. An organization's set of potential customers is referred to as the **market**. Customers interact with the organization to obtain its goods or services. Customers will enter into exchanges with the organization only if they perceive the organization's product or service offerings to be superior to those of the competition (Kotler, 1991, p. 235). To the extent that potential customers perceive the organization's offerings to be superior to the competitors' offerings, and to the extent that these perceptions influence customers over a long period and cannot be easily neutralized or duplicated by competitors, the organization may be said to have *sustainable competitive advantage* in the marketplace.

Product and service offerings include not only tangible products and/or intangible services but also other aspects of the exchange situation. These include issues such as the price and financing arrangement, the location and time the exchange may take place, interpersonal affinity and communication between members of the organization and the customer, and service warranties. The planning and implementation of the offerings and the communication of the offerings to the market through advertising and promotion are the complex activities by which marketing managers create sustainable competitive advantages (Kotler, 1991; Porter, 1980, 1985; Porter and Millar, 1985).

Marketing Activities

We can identify seven general types of activities marketers must carry out to create successful exchange opportunities (Marshall, 1994). These are summarized in Figure 2.1. As the critical first step in developing a marketing program, *marketers must identify potential markets* that can benefit from the possible products of the firm. Such markets must be large enough to represent a real opportunity to contribute to the firm's objectives—usually profitable sales, but not-for-profit organizations may have other objectives (Kotler and Andreasen, 1991; Birks and Southan, 1990). At the same time, marketers must also identify and assess any threats associated with these opportunities.

---

1. Identify potential markets
2. Conceive new products
3. Coordinate with other functional areas of the organization
4. Develop appropriate pricing
5. Develop and coordinate a distribution system
6. Develop effective communication programs
7. Develop ongoing research programs

FIGURE 2.1   Fundamental Marketing Activities

Having identified potential markets, marketers must *conceive of products* (i.e., goods, services, ideas) to meet the needs of these markets. Marketers must then *coordinate with other functional areas in the firm* to ensure that the products are appropriately designed and produced with regard to style, quality, quantity, and so forth, as required by the targeted market. Next, marketers must *develop appropriate pricing*, including financing, and related terms of sale, so that customers can exchange their resources (i.e., cash, credit, or barter) for the product offered by the firm. To ensure that the product is available when and where the potential customer may demand it, *marketers must develop and coordinate a distribution system* to ship the product to appropriate storage facilities, stores, and service locations in the target market so that it can be purchased. With these plans and systems in place, *marketers must develop a communication program* to inform potential customers of the product's availability and how it may be acquired and to stimulate demand by showing how the product can meet potential customers' needs better than competitive products. Finally, because all of these marketing activities require extensive information, the seventh fundamental marketing activity requires that *marketers must carry out ongoing research programs* to provide information to guide the planning and implementation of the six activities described above.

Each of the activities underlying the development of the overall marketing program for an organization requires extensive information. Moreover, the organization is seldom concerned with only a one-time exchange. Instead, it is concerned with creating offers that will be desired by customers on an ongoing basis. Therefore, the information needed to support marketing managers must be provided in a regular, continuous flow. The goal of the MKIS is to provide this ongoing flow of reliable information to support the planning and implementation of the key marketing activities.

Properly carrying out each of these activities will result in the development of a **marketing mix**—the controllable variables an organization puts together to create an offer that will appeal to customers. The marketing mix is also known as the **4 Ps of marketing** (McCarthy, 1960; McCarthy and Perreault, 1993). These are product, price, promotion, and place, where the term *place* refers to the distribution system activities. (If you would like more detail on marketing activities, you can refer to textbooks on marketing and marketing management such as those by Zikmund and d'Amico (1993), Kotler (1991), Pride and Ferrell (1993), McCarthy and Perreault (1993), and Boone and Kurtz (1993)).

Positions and Jobs within Marketing Departments

The functions outlined above suggest the responsibilities of many common positions or sections in the typical organization's marketing department. For example, a *marketing research department*'s duties might include carrying out survey research, monitoring MKIS-related information, identifying potential markets, and assessing the competitive and other environmental circumstances that may influence exchange opportunities. *Product managers*—sometimes called brand managers or market managers—are responsible for developing new products, for coordinating with others to bring these into production, and for proposing and implementing pricing, financing, and distribution arrangements. The *advertising or marketing communications department*'s responsibility is to develop and implement promotional plans. The *sales department* of an organization is usually responsible for developing a salesforce or coordinating distribution channels such as wholesalers and retailers. Finally, the *director of marketing* or *vice-president for marketing* is responsible for coordinating these various activities and, in conjunction with other senior managers, for developing strategic market plans based on information provided by market research, advertising, sales, and product managers. All of these activities must be efficiently and accurately carried out if the firm is to achieve its marketing objectives, and all require sophisticated information drawn from complex databases.

USING INFORMATION FOR COMPETITIVE ADVANTAGE

While information is the key to competitive advantage through marketing, it can also be a two-edged sword. For example, too much data can overwhelm a manager, inaccurate data can lead to wrong conclusions and erroneous decisions, and excessively complex databases will be underutilized. Therefore, to develop an effective marketing information system, the system designer—whether an information systems specialist or a marketing manager—must be able to identify the basic information needs of the marketing managers and top executives who may use the system. System designers must also anticipate future information needs and understand how marketing managers can use information to create competitive advantage.

Because of the extensive and complex information needs of marketers and the broad range of possible information resources, it is helpful to develop a model of types of data that can help marketers. Before we look at these models in detail, let us briefly consider how marketing managers can use different types of information to create competitive advantage.

Internal Information

Marketers benefit greatly from information about the internal operations of the organization. For instance, data on sales patterns allows a sales manager to assess salespeople and can help a marketing manager distinguish among sales problems resulting from salesperson performance, product quality, or unique situations in a geographic territory (Dunne and Wolk, 1977). Information about responses to specific advertisements or promotional programs helps advertising managers select media outlets and choose which advertisements to use in which circumstances. Information on manufacturing costs and processes helps product managers improve product quality and reduce costs. Also, customer service department data can alert the marketer to problems with product quality or design and can suggest new opportunities.

External Information

With proper information about the external environments in which the organization operates, marketing managers can identify and assess **market segments**— groups of potential customers with similar needs or buying characteristics. Information about competitors, for example, helps marketers locate weaknesses in competitors' offerings or distribution systems and thus can suggest ways of serving customers that competitors could not easily copy. Information about consumers' lifestyles or the needs of industrial customers can suggest new products and services and other ways to make the organization's offerings more valuable to the buyer than competitors' products. Information about customers can also help advertising managers develop more cost-effective promotional programs, position the organization's offerings more favorably in the minds of consumers, and assess the effectiveness of an advertising program. Finally, information about geographic distributions of markets and economic and industrial profiles of geographic areas can help sales managers develop sales territories and quotas, plan the size and characteristics of the sales staff, or select locations for stores and offices.

Typical External Environment Information Needs $---->$	Related Marketing Strategy and Mix Elements $<----$	Typical Internal Environment Information Needs
Competitors Market share Products Cost structures Industry structure	Target markets Segments Size Characteristics	Inbound logistics Suppliers Internal prices Storage costs
Technology Product-related Production Communication Information systems	Product designs Distribution systems Salesforce Type of outlets Transport logistics Warehousing	Operations Manufacturing Costs Inventories Finished goods Flexibility Rework costs
Customers Purchase patterns Demographics Psychographics Product requirements Satisfaction	Promotion plans Advertising media Ad content Sales promotions Public relations	Outbound logistics Shipping costs Storage costs Shipping costs
Economic Employment trends Economic projections Disposable income Interest rate trends Exchange rates	Pricing plans Prices Financing terms Channel margins	Sales Product sales Salesperson commisions Geographic area Wholesaler Retailer Commissions
Political Legislation Treaties Elections Regulatory agencies Judicial rulings	Customer services Training Return policies Warranties	Customer service Costs Requests Complaints
Social and cultural Roles/values Religions/belief systems		

FIGURE 2.2   External and Internal Information Requirements of Marketing Managers

These are only a few of the possible uses of information an effective marketing information system can provide, but they show how a MKIS can create opportunities for competitive advantage. With so many opportunities and types of information to choose from, however, the MKIS planner must develop a systematic approach to identifying the types of information that will be helpful. In the next section we will consider two approaches: *internal environmental scanning and analysis,* drawing on Michael Porter's value chain analysis approach to competitive advantage (Porter and Millar, 1985), and *external environmental scanning and analysis*, drawing on the classic model of external marketing environments used by Montgomery and Weinberg (1979). The relation of these paradigms to marketing decision making is depicted in Figure 2.2.

INTERNAL ENVIRONMENTAL MONITORING AND COMPETITIVE ADVANTAGE

The internal environments of a firm are diverse; accordingly, the MKIS planner needs a systematic approach to reviewing information requirements related to the internal operations of the organization. As you may recall, the internal environment consists of all of the activities and circumstances that occur within the organization. One way to identify relevant issues and data on the internal environment is to consider the activities described by Michael Porter (1980, 1985; Porter and Millar, 1985) as the organization's "value chain." By carefully managing the value chain, the firm can create competitive advantages.

The **value chain** is a sequence of activities by which the firm brings raw materials into the organization, processes these into finished products that will be desired by the market, and distributes these to customers. Porter's value chain includes five primary activities by which businesses create value for customers and four support activities. The primary activities are inbound logistics, operations, outbound logistics, marketing and sales, and service. The support activities include the firm's infrastructure, human resource management, technology development, and procurement. All of these activities—the primary activities, in particular—provide a useful checklist for considering internal forces and costs that can direct or constrain an organization's marketing strategy and the elements of the marketing mix. The right-hand column of Figure 2.2 outlines and elaborates these activities as possible sources of data for input to a MKIS. Let's now consider each of these in detail.

Inbound Logistics

Inbound logistics considers how the firm obtains needed resources from the environment and from suppliers. Suppliers' resources and costs affect product development and design, and they influence overall costs for the firm and its specific products. While marketers might not work directly with suppliers, awareness of cost constraints can sensitize the marketer to areas in which products are

---

vulnerable to the competition and can suggest ways to work with suppliers to reduce costs. Similarly, material and storage costs can suggest marketing opportunities or threats, particularly when competitors have better access to supplies or lower costs. With these issues in mind, U.S. automakers such as Chrysler, Ford, and General Motors worked closely with their suppliers in the 1970s and 1980s to develop automated quality control and "just-in-time" inventory systems, which have led to much-improved product quality, product designs, competitive pricing, sales, and profitability.

Production Operations

Information on the *production operations* of the firm also influences marketing programs. For instance, production costs add to a product's variable costs and decrease price flexibility. Limitations on production techniques constrain the marketer's ability to develop new products and improve old products. Product managers must monitor quality control and rework costs so they can assess product designs that might reduce costs, prevent problems from reaching customers, minimize service costs, and increase customer satisfaction. Finally, while high inventory levels suggest the need for special sales promotions to reduce inventory levels, low inventory levels may allow advertising and promotional expenditures to be reduced, at least temporarily.

Outbound Logistics

Well-managed **outbound logistics**—the physical and procedural systems for warehousing goods and transporting them to customers—can also lead to competitive advantage. For example, a marketer should consider the efficiency of physical distribution systems, such as shipping and warehousing costs, because lower physical distribution costs increase pricing flexibility. The importance of outbound logistics goes beyond cost control, however. The product must also be available to the customer when and where he or she desires it. Therefore, data on shipping and inventory records can help the marketer identify customers and the locations of users of products and assess the effectiveness of distribution facilities in serving customer needs.

Marketing and Sales

Internal sales records allow the marketer to monitor unit product sales, prices obtained, and gross margins by product type, geographic area, wholesaler, retailer, and salesperson. A well-organized system for sales records can allow the marketer to monitor sales and allocated costs at each aggregated level of analysis (i.e., by product, retailer, wholesaler, region, country, etc.). For this type of analysis, it may be useful to organize product and sales data as a set of relational databases. Today's scanner data systems have dramatically increased the capabilities of marketers to use such an approach to continually assess product performance and gross margins by distribution channel and store and to monitor store inventories for just-in-time restocking.

Service

Service records are another important source of information for marketing managers who must monitor product quality and customer satisfaction. Service records can suggest how customers use products, the features they value, the types of persons who actually use the product (as compared to the purchaser), and the benefits the user expects. A well-planned system for collecting customer service information can be a particularly valuable way to gather customer information on the success of marketing programs. This is why many companies include warranty registration cards with products.

Black and Decker is one example of a company that used warranty card information to develop a new marketing strategy. Throughout the product planning and development process for its new *Quantum* line of power tools, Black and Decker interviewed customers of earlier products. These customers were identified through warranty cards (Caminiti, 1993). The result was a highly successful new line that achieved rapid acceptance.

EXTERNAL ENVIRONMENTAL SCANNING AND ANALYSIS FOR COMPETITIVE ADVANTAGE

Environmental scanning is the process of monitoring the environment for events that may influence the organization. **Environmental analysis** is the process of assessing and interpreting data gathered by environmental scanning. Both environmental scanning and environmental analysis are aspects of a *strategic intelligence system*. According to Montgomery and Weinberg, a strategic intelligence system should have three purposes: defensive intelligence, passive intelligence, and offensive intelligence (1979, p. 42). **Defensive intelligence** monitors environments to avoid surprises and to verify the organization's assumptions. **Passive intelligence** yields benchmark data on competitors and other environmental forces. **Offensive intelligence** seeks to achieve the organization's goals. To meet its intelligence objectives, the organization must monitor six types of external environments, each of which is shown in the leftmost column of Figure 2.2. These are

- the competitive environment;
- the technological environment;
- customers;
- the economic environment;
- the political environment; and
- the social/cultural environment.

For each of these environments, marketing managers must determine the critical issues and information that need to be monitored. The information to be monitored, in turn, depends on such factors as the nature of the industry, the diversity of the industry's markets, the organization's products, and the organization's strategic objectives. Because decision makers may be overwhelmed by excessive data and because problems of managing and analyzing data become much more difficult as the volume of data increases, it is important to be selective in identifying the appropriate issues and data to monitor. As Montgomery and Weinberg observe, "The problem is not to generate data, but to determine what information is relevant and actionable" (1979, p. 44).

While marketing managers and top executives must ultimately decide what information is relevant and actionable and should be included in the MKIS database, efforts should be made to help *all* managers to be focused and selective in identifying issues and data needs. To put this process into perspective, consider the possible implications of each of the six external environments, paying particular attention to how information related to that environment can help provide competitive advantage.

The Competitive Environment

The **competitive environment** includes the structural features of the industry and the activities and capabilities of competitors (Kotler, 1991, pp. 221–286). Specific issues include such concerns as production costs, economies of scale, extent of product differentiation, capital requirements, distribution channels, and the power of suppliers. Specific competitors' market shares, brand recognition, customer loyalty, and technological advantages should also be studied.

Information on these types of topics can help a marketing manager recognize competitors' strengths and weaknesses and therefore build sustainable competitive advantage. For example, if you know a competitor has high production costs compared to those of your company, then you may be able to use low price as a competitive advantage because the competitor's higher production costs may prevent the competitor from lowering prices without accepting losses. This strategy was used effectively in the U.S. airline industry in the last decade, leading to the defeat of weaker companies in this competitive industry. For another example, suppose your competitor has high levels of brand recognition and customer loyalty. In this situation, you might develop programs that target new market segments to gain competitive advantage rather than attack the competitor head-on. This type of strategy is often used in the soft drink industry when new beverage manufacturers seek to enter the market.

The Technological Environment

The **technological environment** encompasses a wide range of fields in which physical innovations and new ways of carrying out activities can affect business operations and market needs or can create new business opportunities. Companies create competitive advantage and improve their market position by anticipating and adopting new technologies. They also need to know whether their competitors are adopting a new technology that may give them a competitive advantage.

One type of change in the technological environment is inventions that become new products, such as Polaroid cameras, electrostatic printing technologies, or airplanes. Another type of change in the technological environment is improvements in existing technologies. In addition to resulting in new or improved products, technological changes can also create new production technologies that can, in turn, lead to reduced production costs for current products or make product improvements possible. Technological changes can also affect distribution systems, business communications, and the very processes by which business is carried out. Technological changes can even lead to the creation of new competitors and can alter the structure of an industry.

The downfalls of Wang and NBI are examples of how new technologies can revolutionize an industry and lead to the demise of market leaders who failed to understand the implications of the new technologies. In the early 1980s, Wang and NBI were major industry leaders in the high-technology field of office word processing. Both companies had built substantial portions of their business on being at the forefront of this industry. In the early 1980s, these systems were large, difficult to maintain, and expensive. Thus, Wang and NBI's principal markets were corporate customers. By 1983, however, desktop computers and effective word processing software had become available and Wang and NBI began to lose significant market share to their competitors' new, less expensive alternatives. Continued technological improvements in desktop computer speeds and capabilities created growing competition for Wang and NBI. Still these companies did not seem to adapt. By the early 1990s, both companies were largely excluded from the corporate word processing market.

Customers

The **customer environment** includes the organization's current and potential customers. Customers provide product ideas, recommendations for improving distribution systems, and many other suggestions that can help organizations develop competitive advantage. *Fortune* (1993a, 1993b, 1993c) special reports on such successful companies as Black and Decker, Great Plains Software, General Electric, and the Marriot hotel chain illustrate how businesses benefit from close attention to customers. Monitoring your own customers through careful analysis of point-of-sale (POS) scanner data, single-source data systems, customer service, warranty cards, and occasional primary (i.e., original) research studies of customers and noncustomers is a helpful way of building a database of customer information that marketing managers can use in the planning stages of marketing programs and for monitoring the success of ongoing programs. Buyers who choose competitors' products can also suggest ways to gain competitive advantage because they may reveal problems in your product or marketing effort or tell you about a competitor's weakness.

The Economic Environment

Because the medium of exchange for business is financial, economic environments must be monitored. **Economic environments** are the financial and monetary systems that influence the firm and its markets. Today, economic environments are global and the MKIS developer must carefully consider the key indicators of world and domestic economies that can affect her or his organization's business. Developed countries typically have well-organized government and private systems for monitoring, predicting, and reporting economic trends, international monetary exchange rates, and current economic activity. In the United States, private information resources such as the *Survey of Buying Power* (Sales and Marketing Management, 1994) and a variety of information subscription services (Dialog Information Services, 1993; Krol, 1992; Darian, 1989) supplement the public data resources of the U.S. government. Stewart (1984) also offers an extensive list of potential sources. Unfortunately, economic data from less developed countries are often more difficult to obtain, and sources such as the United Nations should not be overlooked.

With proper economic data, the marketer can verify the buying power of prospective markets and ensure that economic investments in marketing activities are well planned and timed. For example, marketers of expensive, high-tech luxury products for the home, such as high-definition televisions, might be reluctant to introduce their products to target markets suffering from high and rising unemployment, exceptionally high consumer debt, and high interest rates. By contrast, markets with high employment and disposable income may be good opportunities for introducing such products.

The Political Environment

The **political environment** consists of government and legal forces that influence business. These include legislation, regulatory agencies, judicial rulings, the threat of legal action, international treaties, tariffs, trade quotas, and even the risk of revolution or changing political parties and leaders. In 1992, meetings between the United States and France regarding oilseed production quotas in the General Agreements on Tariffs and Trade (GATT) treaty led to the threat of high U.S. tariffs on French wines. While oilseed production seemed unrelated to French wine sales, the United States used the threat of tariffs as leverage in negotiations. Had the conflict not been resolved, French wineries might have suffered long-term disadvantages in the U.S. market. This, in turn, would have had negative impacts on United States importers, distributors, and retailers of French wines. Similarly, in mid-1993 confusion existed in trade relations among the United States, Canada, and Mexico due to political uncertainty in the U.S. Congress regarding the North American Free Trade Agreement (NAFTA). Continuing negotiations made it difficult for U.S. companies to plan future business developments until the NAFTA treaty was ratified by the U.S. Congress. The MKIS developer must work with marketing managers to identify such actions and trends in the political environment that may affect the organization and to identify sources of information regarding these.

The Social/Cultural Environment

The **social environment** includes the cultural and demographic characteristics and trends of the markets in which the organization might participate. While *demographic data* such as statistics on population size and on age, racial, and ethnic distributions may be fairly easily obtained for many developed markets, it may be difficult to locate information for specific geographic regions within a country or for less developed regions of the world. Significant cultural characteristics also influence business activities. These include religions, traditional belief systems, customs, language, general lifestyle characteristics, and formal and informal business practices. Shifts in social values and gender roles have had strong influences on sales of automobiles, fast-food, health care, housing, and home entertainment activities in the United States in recent years. While social and cultural factors can affect broad, impersonal markets, these factors can also affect the development of personal relationships that influence buyer behavior in industrial markets.

SUMMARY

The objective of marketing is to create opportunities for exchange in which customers for the organization's products will desire its products and interact with the organization more than with competitor organizations. This is the essence of competitive advantage. Marketers can create competitive advantage in the marketplace by effectively carrying out the seven key activities of marketing listed in this chapter. These activities are

- identifying potential markets;
- conceiving new products;
- coordinating with other functional areas of the organization;
- developing appropriate pricing;
- developing and coordinating a distribution system;
- developing effective communication programs; and
- developing ongoing research programs.

To carry out these activities effectively, marketers need extensive information on a timely basis. Information is needed on the diverse aspects of the external environments in which the organization operates and on the various internal activities of the organization that make up its value chain—that is, the process by which value is added to raw materials as they are transformed into goods and services desired by a market and are distributed to the customers in that market. By providing the information required by marketing managers to support effective decision making, marketing information systems can be a resource for sustainable competitive advantage. In this chapter we have considered various types of data and information that can help marketing managers. We have also considered several examples of how such information can affect marketing programs. With this background, we can better understand the utility of the data resources discussed in Part 2, the decision support systems reviewed in Part 3, and the overall development process presented in Part 4.

Key Terms

4Ps of marketing

boundary department

competitive environment

customer environment

defensive intelligence

economic environments

environmental analysis

environmental scanning

inbound logistics

market

marketing

marketing mix

market segments

offensive intelligence

outbound logistics

passive intelligence

political environment

social environment

sustainable competitive
 advantage

technological environment

value chain

READINGS FOR MORE INFORMATION ON TOPICS IN CHAPTER 2

Deans, C. P., and M. J. Kane (1992). *International Dimensions of Information Systems and Technology.* Boston: PWS-Kent.

Kotler, P. (1991*). Marketing Management: Analysis, Planning, Implementation, and Control* (7th ed.). Englewood Cliffs, NJ: Prentice Hall.

Porter, M. E., and V. E. Millar (1985). "How Information Gives You Competitive Advantage." *Harvard Business Review,* Vol. 63, No. 4 (July/August), pp. 149–160.

Stewart, D. W. (1984). *Secondary Research: Information Sources and Methods.* Newbury Park, CA: Sage.

Zikmund, W. G., and M. d'Amico (1993). *Marketing.* Eagan, MN: West.

Data Resources for Marketing Information Systems

3

Mining the Organization's Internal Data[‡]

[‡] This appendix represents the joint work of Kimball P. Marshall and Roger A. Pick.

In Chapter 2 we cited several examples of the types of internal and external data that are helpful to marketers in their decision making. Now, in Part 2 of this book, we will look more closely at these potential sources of information. Chapter 3 begins the discussion by systematically considering the types of internal data collected at each stage of the value chain. In Chapter 4 we will explore new developments in external data resources, including interorganizational electronic data transfers, single-source data systems, on-line information provided by third-party data vendors, and market research activities. Let us turn now to a discussion of the types of internal data that organizations routinely collect and how this information helps marketing decision making.

Modern businesses know the value of their internal data—information collected by the firm on a regular basis as a routine part of business activities. Internal data is today recognized as having both strategic and tactical value (Campbell, Duperret-Tran, and Campbell, 1994; Gendelev, 1992), and companies in all industries—from banking to motorcycles—are realizing the benefits of applying information technology to activities ranging from quality control to cost containment (Caminiti, 1993; Pare, 1993). Internal data can be thought of as the organization's memory. Like our own memory, it can be used to improve decision making.

Using the Porter value chain analysis model described in Chapter 2 (Porter and Millar, 1985), we will classify data into five general types based on their location in the value chain, as shown in Figure 3.1. These are

- inbound logistics data;
- production and operations data;
- outbound logistics data;
- sales and marketing data; and
- customer service data.

As we consider each of these types of data, keep in mind that exactly what data will be available depends on the individual organization and its data collection procedures. The objective of this chapter is to increase your awareness of the potential gold mine of marketing information that may already be available in an organization so that you will be prepared to seek out this information to support marketing decisions. This background will help you to better understand the activities involved in the MKIS planning and development phases discussed in later chapters. With this in mind, let us consider the first of the five categories of internal data, inbound logistics data.

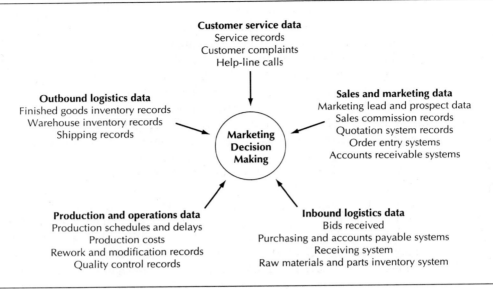

FIGURE 3.1   Types of Internal Data Helpful to Marketers

INBOUND LOGISTICS DATA

As defined earlier, inbound logistics refers to how firms obtain needed resources from the environment and from suppliers. Examples given in Chapter 2 included information from suppliers, as well as internal storage cost data. Other examples of inbound logistics data include contracts between the organization and its suppliers, internal receiving records, records of quality control inspection efforts, and so forth. To illustrate potential sources of inbound logistics data, let's look at three types of internal data systems:

- Purchasing and accounts payable systems
- Receiving systems
- Raw materials and parts inventory systems

Purchasing and Accounts Payable Systems

By **purchasing and accounts payable systems**, we mean the formal procedures for making purchasing decisions, verifying that the proper goods or services have been received, and making payment for those goods or services. Even when the decision-making process is somewhat informal, such as in smaller companies or when purchases are not expensive, there are formal procedures for these activities and formal records to document them. Although such systems are actually designed to provide organizational controls to ensure quality and prevent inefficiency and fraud, the information contained in such systems can also be relevant to marketing managers.

Purchasing and accounts payable information benefits the marketer by identifying suppliers of raw materials and components used in products and by providing information on costs and lead times for delivery of goods and services. For instance, marketers may wish to work as business partners with suppliers who can help identify business trends or plan for future product changes. Cost information can help a marketer understand the constraints his or her other marketing program must consider. Where raw material or component costs appear high, marketing product managers may wish to seek alternative suppliers. Understanding lead times for delivery of goods and services can help marketers plan the timing of a marketing program for introducing a new product or a program to phase out an existing product.

In addition to the information these systems can provide on the costs and performance of actual suppliers, data stored in the purchasing system (even if in written rather than electronic form) may be able to provide information on other suppliers in the industry who are used by competitors. For example, if a supplier your organization rejected was chosen by your competitor, the information contained in the bid your firm rejected may provide helpful hints regarding your competitor's situation.

The Receiving System

The organization's receiving system is also part of inbound logistics. As used here, the **receiving system** is a system of procedures by which an organization accepts a shipment of goods or receives a service and verifies compliance with contract specifications related to the design and quality of the goods or services. As part of their internal environmental scanning efforts, marketers must be kept aware of problems with suppliers. Since marketers are ultimately responsible for the products sold by their organizations, they must monitor the performance of the suppliers of raw materials and component parts. If there is a consistent pattern of delays in receiving expected products or a pattern of failure to meet quality expectations, marketers may wish either to work closely with the supplier to correct these problems or to seek new suppliers.

The Raw Materials and Parts Inventory System

The **raw materials and parts inventory system** is a system used by the production department to ensure that all materials will be on hand to meet production schedules required by marketing's sales forecasts. This type of system should maintain information on a continuous basis regarding the stocks of each part used in a product, the resupply schedule, and estimates of safety stock. **Safety stock** is the minimum amount of a specific part that is to be held in inventory before a new order is issued to replenish the inventory. Marketers must monitor the inventory levels of parts in order to make the best decisions regarding schedules for sales promotions, new product introductions, changes in product designs, and even the deletion of obsolete products from the product line. For example, if a large quantity of a particular part is in the raw materials and parts inventory and that part is used only in a product that marketers are considering deleting, marketers may wish to delay announcing the phaseout of the old product and the introduction of a related new product until the inventory is further depleted.

PRODUCTION AND OPERATIONS

The second stage of the value chain is production and operations. It is in this stage that the raw materials, modules, component parts, and services that were acquired in the inbound logistics stage are transformed into finished goods that the organization will, in turn, ship, store, and sell. Throughout the entire life of the product, but particularly during the early production runs, marketers will benefit from information related to production and assembly problems.

Just as marketers need to be alerted if component materials required for a product are in short supply, they also need to know if production workers are having difficulty in a step in the assembly process. This information is important because such difficulties may lead to unit cost overruns or poor product quality. Similarly, marketers must have information available on rework and modification problems and costs because these may suggest production and product design problems, or even problems in the overall new product development process.

Production and operations issues have their equivalents in retailing and wholesaling environments. In retail stores, for example, the equivalent of production might be the stocking of shelves and the maintenance of a clean store environment. Store marketers must have access to information on shoplifting, goods damaged in the store, and product returns. This information allows retailers to plan product inventories that reduce these problems and to work with manufacturers and wholesalers to develop displays that fit the store atmosphere and do not lead to breakage or theft.

OUTBOUND LOGISTICS

Outbound logistics, as a stage of the value chain, refers to the physical and procedural systems for warehousing goods and transporting them to customers. This includes such activities as (1) monitoring and internal warehousing of finished goods and (2) shipping and external warehousing.

Monitoring and Internal Warehousing of Finished Goods

Warehousing begins as finished goods come off the production line and are stored at the company as part of the finished goods inventory. Because maintaining an inventory costs money and increases business risks, firms must continually monitor the amount of their finished goods by product type so that the level of inventories can be known at any point in time. While the firm will have minimum (safety stock) and maximum inventory levels that are acceptable according to standards established in the management and marketing plans, actual inventories will vary. If managers are kept regularly informed about the amount of finished goods inventory, they can develop more effective tactical plans for sales promotions and better coordinate selling efforts with available products.

High inventory levels for a specific product can suggest a market problem if the production level is not consistent with plans. Low inventory levels, on the other hand, may suggest the risk of lost sales opportunities if the cause is products selling faster than anticipated. In this latter case, the marketer would want to arrange to increase production for fast-selling products. The marketer might also work with the production manager to establish new safety stock standards. When inventory levels reach the new standard, the system automatically begins replenishing the inventory. Such decisions, however, would also have to consider the impacts of production schedule changes on all other products.

Shipping and External Warehousing

Shipping and external warehousing make up the physical distribution system. These activities involve physically moving goods to an off-site warehouse, to a member of the sales distribution channel (a wholesaler, retailer, or industrial distributor who will resell the product), to a company sales branch, or to a customer. The goals of physical distribution systems are to reduce costs and increase customer service (Pride and Ferrell, 1993, p. 438). Effective and efficient distribution systems require an "optimal" plan for the type of shipping services and routes to use, as well as the locations of *field warehouses*—warehouses outside the company's factories—and the amounts of inventory to be maintained in those facilities. These decisions can dramatically affect distribution costs and the availability of products to customers. For instance, IKEA, a Swedish manufacturer of ready-to-assemble furniture, has used innovative approaches to developing distribution centers in the United States to ensure that its products are readily available to customers while it develops new retail outlets.

When a product is ready to be shipped, the services of a shipping company—also called a *common carrier*—must be arranged. As part of the shipping process, a *bill of lading*—in essence, a purchase order for a transportation service—is prepared. Information about the bill of lading is passed to the accounts payable system so that the firm will be prepared to pay the carrier's bill when it is presented. The information on the bill of lading includes the name of the shipper, the destination, the name of the person to receive the shipment, the origin, the product shipped, the terms of ownership, and the shipping costs.

This information may be useful to marketing managers because there are cases in which a firm sells a product to an intermediary (i.e., a wholesaler or retailer) but ships it directly to the customer. If only the order entry record is considered, the actual customer (who is also the final purchaser) might be overlooked. Even when sales intermediaries are purchasing the product from the company, it is important for an organization to know who the actual end user will be and to seek to satisfy that person.

Shipping information can affect marketing planning in other ways as well. The time from the entry of an order to shipment may be very important to potential customers, and marketers may want to work to improve this time. Shipping records can indicate whether a carrier is reliable or has a high risk of being late or of losing or damaging cargos. Effective marketing management requires that such issues be monitored so that appropriate steps can be taken to improve quality and customer satisfaction. Both IBM and Xerox built their reputations as leaders in their industries in part on their abilities to rapidly respond to customer needs in a reliable manner.

SALES, MARKETING, AND SERVICE

Sales and marketing, and customer service activities, make up the fourth and fifth steps of the value chain. They are the crucial links between your organization and its customers. Sales and customer services activities can generate a great deal of information about who your market is, where it is, how large it is, how it can be reached, what customers think of you, and how to improve. Sales and service systems might be described in any number of ways. For our purposes, we have chosen to order a series of steps extending from a salesperson seeking out leads and prospects to the fulfillment of an order to the customer's satisfaction.

In this section we will describe each step in the sales and customer service processes and their related information systems activities. Each of these activities can generate marketing-relevant information. These stages are

- lead and prospect systems;
- quotation systems;
- order entry;
- sales commissions;
- accounts receivable systems; and
- service.

Lead and Prospect Systems

The benefits of lead and prospect systems for improving marketing programs have generated growing interest in these types of systems among companies as diverse as American Express, Philip Morris, Seagram & Sons, General Motors, Blockbuster Entertainment, and Harley-Davidson (*Business Week*, September 5, 1994). These companies use responses to the database marketing capabilities of lead and prospect systems to help them plan and direct promotional campaigns and carry out market research activities that influence decisions affecting market segmentation, product designs, and advertising messages.

Lead and prospect tracking systems are procedures for generating **leads**— names and ways of contacting potential customers who may have an interest in a product—qualifying that lead as a **prospect**—a lead worthy of contact—and tracking the outcome of contacts. These systems can be as simple as a personal computer data file maintained by an insurance agent or as complex as the multimillion-dollar system maintained by American Express. Even a salesperson's daily, weekly, or monthly activity reports can provide useful lead information. While some organizations develop their own systems, a large number of commercial software vendors offer a wide range of products with great flexibility in capabilities (Datapro, 1989).

Lead tracking systems typically include a database subsystem that contains names, addresses and phone numbers, and perhaps some demographic, industrial, psychographic, or social information. The system may also include some form of *lead interview schedule*, in which a salesperson presents a product idea to the lead and explores the lead's interest. The system may even include the ability to forward prospects to outside salespeople for follow-up, to mail additional information, or to remind the lead system operator to recontact the lead at a future time.

At least two types of information useful to marketers can be developed from lead and prospect system data. First, contacts with leads provide opportunities to gather information on what different types of potential customers need and what types of products and features they want. Information in the lead database can be statistically analyzed to identify market segments that respond favorably to certain products or to certain types of offers.

A second form of information that lead and prospect systems can provide is data to assess the effectiveness of advertising and sales promotion programs. Leads that result from certain advertisements, for example, can allow marketers to estimate more accurately the cost-benefit per lead of advertising in certain magazines. A company might use a special 800 number on an advertisement in one magazine and a second phone number in another magazine. Monitoring the number of calls to each phone number may suggest the relative effectiveness of advertising in each magazine.

The value of lead and prospect systems has not been lost on Dell Computers (*Fortune*, 1993a). Dell invests over $50 million per year in information technology, much of it focused on supporting its direct sales system. Dell officials estimate that they receive over 35,000 calls per day, including electronic-mail messages, from potential customers seeking sales and product information or customer service. Data from these calls is recorded on computer systems as it is received, and the information is stored and analyzed. Tom Martin, a Dell marketing manager, remarked to *Fortune* that Dell's marketing personnel are so attuned to its response tracking system that they know a mailer using a yellow background will get a 30 percent lower response rate than a mailer using a gray background!

Sales and lead information helped Dell increase the response rate for its small-business mailings by 250 percent, and the information generated from these and other customer information systems is used to guide salespeople who contact customers, as well as product developers who plan new offers.

Quotation Systems

A **quote** is a promise to deliver a good or service by a stated time for a stated price. In its simplest form, **quotation preparation** involves an offer to deliver a specified product or service to a customer, at a specified price, location, and time. For direct sales or bids on complex products, quotation preparation may involve assembling a document of hundreds or thousands of pages. Such complex quotations are usually called *proposals*.

The first task for a quotation system is to determine what product is of interest to the customer. After verifying that the product corresponds to a good or service the firm markets, the quotation system ensures product availability by ascertaining (1) if the good is in inventory and not yet committed by other quotations; (2) if production has already been scheduled for the good (for resellers, this would correspond to assuming sufficient quantities of goods or orders) and, if so, when the finished good will be available; or (3) when the production or purchasing systems will be able to schedule delivery of the product.

After the system has ascertained that the firm can fulfill the potential order, the system determines the price. This involves looking up the value from a table but often also has to include volume discounts, sales promotions, and geographic variations that may affect price, shipping charges, or other factors specified in marketing's pricing guidelines.

Quotation systems can tell marketers who is a customer and who is not. Even a quote that does not result in a sale yields important information about sources of customers and customer needs and wants. It is similarly important to analyze customer lists to identify customers who have stopped buying and gone to competitors. Further contacts with these former customers and their salespeople may uncover the reasons they left the company. Customers who have switched to another supplier might be wooed back, and knowledge of why they left the company can help the firm to avoid losing other customers. For example, Patricia Sellers (1993) reports that MicroScan, a medical instruments supplier, discovered it was losing customers because it did not have a particular type of analytical equipment that was comparable to a competitor's product. As a result of this information, the company developed a new product within eighteen months and in 1992 captured 70 percent of its industry's new equipment sales.

Order Entry

When a lead becomes a prospect and then makes a purchase, the order entry step begins. **Order entry** is the set of procedures by which an order is placed in a form that can be handled by the firm's processing systems. Order entry requires customer identification and determination of payment terms, as well as specification of the products ordered, the quantities, and prices. The goal of order entry is to obtain this information as easily as possible. A recent trend in order entry involves providing information systems that "empower customers to serve themselves" (Rice, 1993, p. 51). One widespread example of such a system is retail banking and the automatic teller machine. Other examples include self check-in at airlines, rental car counters, and hotels.

Customer identification is relatively simple for repeat customers. When the identifying information is entered into the system, it verifies whether this information corresponds to a customer already on file. For new customers or customers whose records require updating, customer identification involves determining who the customer is, checking credit-worthiness, and obtaining billing and shipping addresses. Typical customer information might include name, billing address, shipping address, day and evening telephone numbers, and payment information (such as credit card number). The name of the responsible salesperson should also be recorded, and, if the customer is a business, a purchase order number is usually necessary as well.

Following customer identification, items being purchased and their quantities must be entered into the system. Items are often entered using a unique item number or product code, which must be validated. A valid item number corresponds to an actual good or service in a look-up table maintained on the order entry computer system.

If the prices to be charged for each item are standardized, they may be automatically inserted in the order entry record by the computer system, perhaps using the same look-up table that was used to verify the product code. If special conditions exist and the pricing is not standard, the special price and the reason why it is being charged may have to be entered.

The information gathered during order entry can provide insights into what sorts of customers buy the firm's goods or services. Addresses, especially zip codes, can be analyzed to learn if customers are geographically concentrated and where. The social and demographic characteristics of these locations can be used to identify other, demographically similar areas in which to target promotional efforts. Dell Computer (*Fortune*, 1993a) stores the data from its 35,000 daily customer contacts and uses this information to increase the effectiveness of its direct mailings by tailoring them to specific market niches.

Sales Commissions

Sales commission records keep track of the sales staff's performance. If sales representatives are paid by commission, bonuses, or any other form of compensation tied to individual sales, the necessary information must be gathered at order entry time. Otherwise, the data becomes difficult to obtain. Thus, as we mentioned above, each order should identify the salesperson responsible for the sale. Later, the information for each salesperson can be combined to compute sales commissions and to allow performance evaluations. This information could also be matched to other data in the salesperson's file to allow summary information for branch offices or regional offices to be calculated and reported. Similar kinds of totals can be computed to determine sales of individual products, sales for individual product lines, sales for an entire line of business, and sales by region, distribution channel, or price break. The data represented by all the individual transactions within a firm would overwhelm the manager who looks at them. However, when this volume of data is reduced by calculating totals or averages for meaningful subgroups, the manager can understand the information within that volume of data and gain the consequent insights.

Accounts Receivable Systems

Accounts receivable systems keep track of which customers owe how much money for what goods and services. The major subfunctions are invoicing, billing, receiving payment, and correcting entries. When a customer receives a good or service, the customer becomes legally obligated to pay for it. *Invoicing* is the process of determining how much the customer owes and informing the customer of the obligation. *Billing* is a periodic reminder of a debt. When a customer pays, the system must match the payment to the customer and reduce that customer's obligation accordingly. *Correcting entries* is necessary to fix errors and to handle returns and back-billing. The reports developed by accounts receivable systems include invoices, periodic statements, and reports for credit managers regarding overdue accounts.

The data saved in the accounts receivable system includes invoices, information about customers, and payments. Invoice files will at the very least contain information to identify the customer, the goods or services delivered, the time of delivery, and the total amount of money owed for the purchase. Customer files generally include the identification information mentioned earlier: name, address, telephone, and payment or credit information. Payment files include data on the customer, the date, the amount, the invoice or order number and payment terms.

There are two major approaches to billing and cash receipt: open-item systems and balance forward systems. With an **open-item system**, the firm keeps track of every invoice sent, and payments are matched to individual invoices. With a **balance forward system**, the firm keeps track only of the total amount the customer owes; payments serve to reduce that total. The main difference between the two types of systems is that individual transaction detail is preserved for a longer time with the open-item system.

Service

Service is the last step of the value chain as presented by Porter. **Customer service systems** are designed with the primary goals of tracking problems customers have with an organization's products and of arranging procedures to correct the problem so as to satisfy the customer. Although the primary and overriding goal must be customer satisfaction, information about customer complaints and product problems—and about effective solutions to those problems—can also help marketers design better products and programs. For example, Terence Pare (1993) describes how customer feedback through the Hewlett-Packard customer support system led to the development of the PerView networking software. It seems that while customers felt that the original product did what it was supposed to do, they wanted it to do more. Hewlett-Packard responded with the new, improved software and increased sales and customer satisfaction.

Peters and Austin (1985) describe a large number of situations in which staying close to customers through marketing and top management involvement in customer support and service has led to business success. They describe, for example, how Apple Computer, in the early 1980s, required executives to spend time each month observing their customer support telephone workers and gave executives special recognition if they actually spoke with customers.

A customer service information system might be designed to obtain information on the product, the dealer or salesperson who sold the product, the nature of the problem, and the familiarity of the user with the product or similar products. Such a system might be designed to provide statistical summaries of types of problems in order to alert marketers to design flaws and to allow marketing managers to read detailed text descriptions of the customer's problem as told to the service operator. Even reports of field service technicians can be monitored in a similar way.

The results of analyzing customer service records may be new product designs, new user instructions, or perhaps new sales training programs to teach salespeople the correct applications for a product. Such analyses may also reveal information about the actual purchasers of products—their buying behavior, product needs, and real-world applications and the features and product improvements they would most value. To achieve these benefits, the designers of customer service systems and the proponents of marketing information systems must work together to develop procedures to collect and store useful data and to make the data available to marketers for analysis.

SUMMARY

The typical firm is rich in internal data resources that can benefit marketing activities and aid marketing decision making. The internal activities by which an organization adds value to raw materials to produce products for customers offer great opportunities to collect and record business operations data that will benefit market planning and the operational management of marketing activities.

Now that we have reviewed many of the major internal sources of data that should be considered for planning a marketing information system, we can turn our attention to external data sources—sources of information that are outside the organization. This is the topic of the next chapter.

Key Terms

accounts receivable systems	open-item system	quote
balance foward system	order entry	raw materials and parts
customer service systems	prospect	inventory system
lead and prospect tracking systems	purchasing and accounts payable systems	receiving system
leads	quotation preparation	safety stock
		sales commission records

Bradley, S. P., J. A. Hausman, and R. L. Nolan (1993). *Globalization, Technology, and Competition: The Fusion of Computers and Telecommunications in the 1990s.* Boston: Harvard University Press.

Business Week (1994). "Database Marketing." *Business Week*, No. 3388 (September 5), pp. 56–62.

Datapro Reports (1989). *Marketing Information Systems.* New York: McGraw-Hill.

Gray, J., and A. Reuter (1993). *Transaction Processing: Concepts and Techniques.* San Mateo, CA: Morgan Kaufmann.

Rochester, J. B. (1992). "Computer/Telephone Integration for Marketing Information Systems." *I/S Analyzer*, Vol. 30 (June), pp. 1–10.

4

External MKIS Data Sources‡

‡ This appendix represents the joint work of Kimball P. Marshall and Roger A. Pick.

Organizations are open systems that enter into exchanges with their environment. Marketing is at the center of these exchanges. If marketing managers are to develop effective programs to facilitate exchanges that will achieve the organization's goals, a systematic and planned program for environmental scanning and analysis is required (Blattberg, Glazer, and Little, 1994; Carroll, 1992). Fortunately, more environmental and customer information is available than ever before (Bessen, 1993). Whereas in Chapter 2 we considered the various types of environments marketers must monitor—competitors, technology, customers, economic, political, and sociocultural—in this chapter we will consider the sources of this marketing-related environmental data. Our goal is to familiarize you with the range of possible sources so that you will be able to consider how they might benefit marketing decision making in the MKIS planning process. The sources we will discuss in this chapter are

- exchanges with business partners;
- marketing environment data subscription services;
- single-source data services; and
- marketing research projects.

These are presented in Figure 4.1.

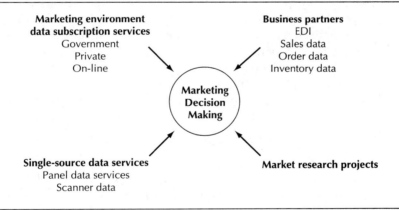

FIGURE 4.1 **Types of External MKIS Data Sources**

Before addressing the first of these sources, we need to point out some important differences between working with internal and external data. With internal data, the organization is in a better position to control what data will be collected and archived, the data's quality, and how the data will be recorded for computer purposes. With external data, on the other hand, the organization may have little control over what information will be available, what its quality will be, or what computer format will be used to record the information. Further complicating the situation is that the organization may have to use multiple sources for the environmental data it desires and even then may need to carry out periodic market research projects to supplement the routinely available data. To address these issues, the organization's information systems department may have to devote considerable attention to developing effective methods for bringing external information into the organization in a format or style that can be read by the MKIS and maintained in the MKIS database.

Despite the problems, however, external data is an indispensable resource. Without external data, the organization cannot plan an effective marketing program, judge its performance against competitors' performances, or adapt to environmental changes. Aware of the challenges, let us now explore the various sources of external data, beginning with data provided by business partners.

EXCHANGES WITH BUSINESS PARTNERS

Business partners are companies involved in the value chain with whom the organization has or expects to have a formal relationship. This relationship may involve supplying products, transporting and warehousing goods, selling goods, and providing customer services. We have already observed how information from suppliers, as well as distribution channel members such as retailers and wholesalers, is important to marketing decision making. Today more than ever, close electronic relationships are being established among business partners to facilitate rapid sharing of information (Rubenstein, 1989; Cash and Konsynski, 1985; O'Callaghan, Daufman, and Konsynski, 1992; Wiseman, 1985, 1988).

Electronic Data Interchanges (EDI)

Electronic data interchanges (EDI), the transmission of standard business documents, can speed sales activities, make just-in-time inventory systems possible among manufacturers, and allow automatic reordering systems by which manufacturers restock retailers and wholesalers. Sophisticated EDI systems can cement strategic alliances among business partners and transform the structure of an industry (Cash et al., 1992, 1993). Of course, businesses can share information without EDI, but EDI speeds the process dramatically—sometimes from days to minutes—routinizes data sharing, and greatly reduces the risk of error, since data transferred by EDI need not be rekeyed into the receiving firm's computer system.

To better understand how EDI applies to marketing decision making, let's look at an example of how manufacturers and retail stores might benefit from EDI. Consider a discount retailer that occupies large stores but maintains very little warehouse space. All purchases in this retailer's stores are processed through cash registers that are also point-of-sale (POS) computer systems. As products are purchased, universal product codes (*UPC codes*), a vendor's *SKU numbers* (identification codes used in warehousing and wholesale and retail trade), or other product codes are entered into the register along with the quantity. This information might be entered by a cash register clerk or more rapidly recorded through automatic identification scanning systems that use bar codes to record transactions. In either case, the result is an ongoing data file that can reveal store inventories at almost any moment. When a store's inventory of a particular item is depleted to the safety stock level, the store's computer system automatically contacts the wholesaler's or manufacturer's computer system to replenish the supply of the product.

It is clear from this example that sharing of business data can make physical distribution systems more efficient. In addition, it can also provide marketers with a variety of other types of critical information needed to maintain competitive advantage. Inventory and sales information shared among business partners can tell marketing product managers how well a new product is being accepted, or it may allow advertisers to assess the sales impact of a new ad campaign or a coupon promotion (Curry, 1993). Such information may even allow a marketer to assess how products are being affected by a competitor's new product or promotion campaign. Similarly, service records of a retailer or industrial distributor can help marketers identify a product's weakness or can stimulate ideas for new products or services.

Issues to Consider When Implementing EDI

To be effective and provide competitive advantage, data sharing through EDI must be carefully implemented. EDI requires a set of standards for how the information that makes up certain documents commonly used in business—a purchase order, for example—can be stored in an electronic record and transmitted. There must also be agreed-upon standards for what can be transmitted and the format of this transmission. Several standards organizations, professional organizations, and industrial trade associations have developed standards for many documents, including requests for quotations, purchase orders, order confirmations, bills of lading, invoices, and checks. These voluntary standards provide a basis from which organizations wishing to pursue EDI can begin to work together.

Interfaces to Existing Transaction Processing Systems

Once a firm and its business partners agree to develop EDI capabilities, the firms involved must adapt their systems to work with the agreed-upon standards while at the same time maintaining the old procedures to accommodate business partners that are not on the EDI system. This involves changes to systems that process information originating outside the firm and changes to systems that send data outside the firm. Systems that formerly accepted data keyed in by a clerk at a terminal must now be adapted to accept data from the EDI network. In some instances, this change might require developing a new program to convert the EDI data into the format that the original data entry program produced. Similarly, programs that produced only printed documents must now be supplemented with programs that will write output into computer records that fit the EDI standards.

Although EDI can be accomplished through direct communication between a firm's computers and its business partners' computers, it is often conducted through *EDI network vendors*, who coordinate transfers among business partners. The EDI network vendor can serve as a "mail drop" of sorts, receiving and forwarding to a firm all of the EDI records that have been sent to it from its business partners, and also receiving and forwarding all the records that the firm wishes to send to its EDI partners. By coordinating the data communications activities among the business partners, the EDI network vendor guarantees accurate electronic delivery of documents without disrupting any of the business partners' information systems.

MARKETING ENVIRONMENT DATA SUBSCRIPTION SERVICES

In Chapter 2 we stressed the benefits of environmental scanning and analysis. The benefits of environmental data are so great that many companies and government agencies actively supply almost every business sector with data on demographic, economic, technological, social, political, and competitive activities (Blattberg, Glazer, and Little, 1994). Whereas in the past such data was provided only in printed form as either statistical tables or formal reports, today data is often available as either on-line computer files or files on diskette, computer tape, or CD-ROM (U.S. Department of Commerce, 1993; O'Brien, 1990). Three types of suppliers of marketing environment data should be considered:

- Government agencies
- Private data vendors
- On-line data services

Government Agencies

The U.S. Department of Commerce is one of the largest suppliers of data on business environments. Such data resources as the U.S. population census (conducted every ten years), the censuses of industries (carried out every five years), and a variety of interim surveys are available on computer tape, CD-ROM, and diskette, or on-line through the Internet (Krol, 1992) to help businesses track demographic, social, and business trends (U.S. Bureau of the Census, 1993).

Other marketing environment data can be found in the publication series *County Business Patterns* (U.S. Bureau of the Census, 1989), for example. This series provides detailed information on the number of employees, sales, and payrolls for industries by Standard Industrial Classification codes (*SIC codes*) for each state and county and for the United States as a whole. The *Census of Manufacturers*, which is updated every five years, provides detailed information on the value of shipments, numbers of production workers, wages, and costs of materials for specific industries. Such information can be used by marketers to compute industry benchmarks from which to evaluate their own company's performance.

In addition to these especially helpful resources, the Department of Commerce frequently carries out special studies of specific industries and issues related to international trade. Similarly, other offices of the U.S. government often provide data as well as on-line news of importance to members of the industries they regulate or are mandated to support.

Finally, individual state and local governments, as well as foreign governments, international agencies, and the United Nations, often provide useful information on marketing environments (Stewart, 1984). Unfortunately, these resources are often less well developed than those supplied by the U.S. government (Ramachandran, 1991).

Private Data Vendors

Private data vendors of marketing-related environmental data—those that are not part of government agencies—include such well-known organizations as Arbitron, AT&T, Citicorp, A. C. Nielsen, and Donnelley (O'Brien, 1990). While much data from the U.S. government is available free or at low cost, data subscription services offered by private vendors may be expensive. In trade, however, private vendors are often willing to work with clients to provide information tailored to their specific needs. For example, Perreault (1992, pp. 370–371) has reported that pharmaceutical firms can subscribe to detailed data on the prescription behavior of individual doctors. While the data available from subscription sources might not always precisely fit the problem or categories desired by marketers, the more difficult problem for marketers may actually be how to identify from the plethora of available sources exactly what information will be helpful.

On-line Data Services

Special attention should be given to computerized on-line data services such as Dialog (Darian, 1989; Johnson, 1989; Dialog Information Systems, 1993), CompuServe (Bowen, 1994), Prodigy (Kane, 1991), and America Online (Lichty, 1993). **On-line data services** serve as clearinghouses and communications networks for on-line data resources drawn from government, trade associations, and many private data collection agencies (Lichty, 1993). A similar but more sophisticated resource that is especially well suited for studying the characteristics of geographically defined target market areas has been developed by National Decisions Systems (Winters, 1990).

Support staff at these organizations can help to identify databases that will provide useful information for marketers. Once a subscriber to these services has identified a useful database, he or she can often transfer data from the service's computer system to his or her own system. If the data must be accessed regularly, the subscriber may be able to have his or her own computer system automatically connect to the service's system at a specified time and download the updated information.

Despite the current popularity of on-line data services, many obstacles still exist to easily incorporating on-line subscription data into a well-designed MKIS database. For instance, after data has been transmitted to the subscriber organization's computer system, the resulting file must be verified to ensure that the correct data was received and that the integrity of the data is intact. Even if the data that was transferred was originally organized into a systematic format so that all data items could be identified, there is some risk that one or more data items may have been lost in transmission or that unexpected computer codes may have been inserted by the computer communications program. There is even the possibility that the subscription service may have changed the layout or contents of the file without notifying the subscriber. Therefore, before transferred data is used for decision making, it is important for procedures to be in place and followed to ensure that the transferred information is checked and accurate.

SINGLE-SOURCE DATA SERVICES

Single-source data services are one of the most rapidly growing areas of marketing information services, particularly among consumer products firms that sell through food stores, drugstores, and mass merchandisers (Curry, 1993; Malhotra, 1992; Overhultz, 1993; Perreault, 1992; Prince, 1990; Peters, 1990). **Single-source data services** are companies that track an individual customer's purchases and link this information to store data, product promotion data, neighborhood data, and other socioeconomic data that describe the consumer and the purchaser. Typically, these projects are conducted over several years in carefully selected test markets. The term *single-source* is used because the process of collecting the diverse data items and providing the comprehensive data set is carried out within one company. The resulting data sets are also referred to as **consumer scanner panel data** because a group of consumers—a *panel*—participates in the research over a long period and because the purchase data is collected using point-of-sale automatic identification scanner systems.

The benefits of consumer scanner panel data can be enormous. Data from consumer panels has allowed marketers to develop statistical models of consumers' brand choice behavior (Guadagni and Little, 1983) and to quickly test new products and other changes in the marketing mix (Perreault, 1992). Other studies have used these systems to help define target markets in terms of shopping behavior (Ingram, 1992). Monitoring consumer scanner information can also help a company respond quickly to market changes that might otherwise have gone unnoticed and can provide data to model competitor reactions to market changes (Leeflang and Wittink, 1992). Bessen (1993) has reported on A&P food stores' use of scanner data to personalize store inventories to customer shopping preferences.

Despite the benefits, single-source data is not without difficulties. One problem is that consumer scanner panel data projects that intend to be comprehensive are fairly capital-intensive and require vast information processing capacities. Furthermore, a relatively long time is needed to collect panel data. This is why only a few companies dominate this field. The largest and most established are Information Resources, Inc. (Liesse, 1993; Harvard Business School, 1982, 1983), Arbitron/SAMI (Wolfe, 1990), Nielsen, AT&T, and Citicorp (O'Brien, 1990).

In addition, there is a risk that the consumer panel members might not be representative, since they must volunteer to be included and must be willing to provide much information. Also, panelists' behavior might be influenced by the knowledge that they are being observed. As Metzger notes (1990), in some cases only about 10 percent of randomly selected subjects have agreed to participate. But these problems are common to many longitudinal panel studies, and single-source data—as well as other types of sales data based on scanner and automatic identification systems—are important to marketing managers today and will become more so in the future (Overhultz, 1993). Larger challenges are the need to develop (1) methods of managing the massive and ever-growing volume of data that single-source vendors can provide and (2) practical analytical models that real-world marketing managers can use.

MARKET RESEARCH PROJECTS

Among marketing researchers, a distinction is often made between marketing research and marketing information systems. Sometimes the term *marketing intelligence system* is used for what we refer to here as a marketing information system (Kotler, 1991). Recall that the goal of a marketing information system, as defined in this book, is to provide an ongoing flow of relevant data to support marketing decision making. The types of marketing-relevant data that we have discussed in this and the previous chapter, for instance, are generally data collected on an ongoing basis.

Marketing research activities also provide data to support marketing decision making and might cover any of a wide range of topics and applications, from product or brand preferences to psychographic or demographic factors associated with store selection. What distinguishes marketing research from MKIS, however, is that marketing research is intended to provide in-depth information collected over a fixed, relatively short time frame (Malhotra, 1992; Churchill, 1991; Williams, 1966). Findings from market research projects supplement the internal and external types of data previously discussed. They allow marketers to look more closely at situational and psychological factors that may underlie changes in market trends uncovered by environmental scanning and analysis. But market research projects cannot take the place of systems to monitor internal and external environments or to monitor consumer purchasing patterns over extended periods.

Because marketing research is either carried out or commissioned by the marketing organization, the organization has more control over the types, quality, and format of the data than with other forms of external data. Furthermore, the data management problem is greatly reduced by the fact that the data is collected over a relatively short time and thus there is no need to build a system of routinized, ongoing data collection.

From a MKIS standpoint, the major technical problem presented by market research data is how to archive such data. Each project is unique, and the data must usually be interpreted within the context of the research situation, goals, and data collection instruments. Therefore, the MKIS database plan should include procedures for archiving market research data while allowing the data to be accessed by marketing managers. The plan must also include a method for archiving the detailed descriptions of the methodological procedures used for data collection and any special circumstances that must be used in interpreting data. Ideally, such documentation would be available on-line for analysts to review on an as-needed basis.

SUMMARY

As the wealth of data available to marketing decision makers continues to explode with technological advances making data collection and dissemination easier, the challenge for MKIS developers is to work with marketing managers to identify what data will be needed and helpful to decision making. As we can see from our review of external data sources—business partners; data subscription services, including government agencies, private vendors, and on-line services; single-source vendors; and market research projects—it is clear that the problem is not locating resources. Instead, the difficulty is knowing how to select and manage resources so that the data can be used by marketing managers on an ongoing basis. Approaches to solving this problem are discussed later in this book in the chapters that address planning, developing, and implementing MKIS systems.

There is another type of problem as well: how to analyze the data brought into the MKIS in order to generate information that will guide decision making. With the familiarity we now have with internal and external data resources, we can begin to consider systems for reporting and analyzing data to guide decision making. This includes consideration of inquiry and reporting systems, as well as decision support systems, expert systems, and artificial intelligence systems. These tools for analyzing marketing data are the topics of Part 3.

Key Terms

business partners	electronic data interchanges (EDI)	on-line data services
consumer scanner panel data	marketing research	private data vendors
		single-source data services

READINGS FOR MORE INFORMATION ON TOPICS IN CHAPTER 4

Bessen, Jim (1993). "Riding the Marketing Information Wave." *Harvard Business Review*, Vol. 71, No. 5 (September–October), pp. 150–160.

Blattberg, R. C., R. Glazer, and J.D.C. Little (Eds.). (1994). *The Marketing Information Revolution*. Boston: Harvard Business School Press.

Cash, J. I., R. G. Eccles, N. Nohria, and R. L. Nolan (1993). *Building the Information Age Organization: Structure, Control, and Information Technologies*. Homewood, IL: Irwin.

Curry, David J. (1993). *The New Marketing Research Systems*. New York: Wiley.

Wiseman, Charles (1988). *Strategic Information Systems*. Homewood, IL: Irwin.

Decision Support Systems and Artificial Intelligence in Marketing

5

Decision Support Systems for Marketing‡

‡ This appendix represents the joint work of Kimball P. Marshall and Roger A. Pick.

The decisions that marketing managers must make are becoming more and more complex. In large part, this is because the growing volume of data available to them makes it increasingly difficult to focus on the most relevant and useful data and to analyze this data to the organization's best advantage. As the decisions become more difficult, marketing managers need help making the most effective and efficient use of the available data to support marketing decisions (Little, 1990). Information systems professionals are helping marketers make the best use of the available data in two ways. First, they are developing MKIS databases that draw on the various internal and external data resources we discussed in the preceding section. Second, they are developing decision support systems and artificial intellegence systems, the topics of this and the next chapter.

In this chapter we will first review the history of decision support systems and consider their characteristics. We will then devote the majority of the chapter to discussing four broad types of decision support systems. In order of complexity and presentation, these types are

- reporting and inquiry systems;
- analytical models for forecasting, simulation, and optimization;
- executive support systems; and
- group decision support systems.

We will devote Chapter 6 to a detailed discussion of a fifth type of decision support system, artificial intelligence systems. These are depicted in Figure 5.1.

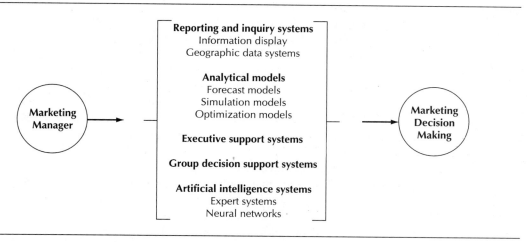

FIGURE 5.1   Types of Decision Support Systems

A **decision support system (DSS)** is the set of "problem-solving technology consisting of people, knowledge, software, and hardware successfully wired into the management process" (Little, 1979) to facilitate improved decision making by marketing managers. Although the DSS concept has been around for nearly two decades, marketers have been slow to adopt these systems, principally because sophisticated systems are often expensive to develop and their impact on the bottom line is difficult to quantify (Eisehart, 1990). Costs and benefits are especially problematic in marketing because the success of a marketing program is affected by many internal and external forces simultaneously. Nonetheless, academic reports and the business, marketing, and information systems trade press indicate that the use of decision support systems in marketing is increasing rapidly (Blattberg, Glazer, and Little, 1994).

This increase may be attributed to several factors. First, as we have already noted, more data is available to marketing managers than ever before and this volume of data requires computer support. Second, computerization of business activities and electronic data interchanges have greatly speeded marketing processes and require increasingly more rapid and effective decisions. Third, rapid increases in the capabilities of computer systems—particularly in desktop computer systems—and the development of user-friendly, fourth-generation language (4GL) software packages that allow information systems specialists and end users to create specialized applications have reduced the costs and time required for development.

DSS applications have not developed evenly in all business sectors, however. The widest adoption of DSS for marketing appears to be in the area of consumer packaged goods, while industrial product companies and service industries have lagged behind (Mohan and Holstein, 1994; Sisodia, 1992; Rothfeder et al., 1990). The early emergence of DSS-type applications for consumer goods, especially in food goods (Ingram, 1992), may be a natural by-product of the data-intensive nature of the sales, warehousing, and distribution channels of retail products (Lodish, 1982). In contrast, industrial product firms have often collected little formal marketing information. Exacerbating the dilemma, information that was collected by industrial product firms was often product- or financials-oriented, not customer- or market-oriented.

O'Brien (1990) notes that competitive pressures lead more marketers to use decision support systems to improve marketplace effectiveness. Given the importance of data availability and customer orientation as impetuses for developing marketing DSS and the shift of companies in many industries to a focus on the customer and a desire to be "fast, flexible, and responsive to competition" (Mohan and Holstein, p. 239), it appears that O'Brien's statement is correct and the field of marketing DSS will grow rapidly.

CHARACTERISTICS OF DECISION SUPPORT SYSTEMS

A DSS is characterized by three features (Bonczek, Holsapple, and Winston, 1981, p. 18):

1. Incorporating models

2. Providing information to higher-level management to support unstructured decisions

3. Providing users with powerful yet simple-to-use languages for problem solving

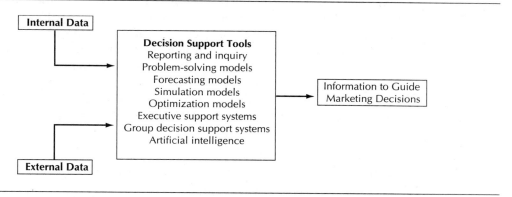

FIGURE 5.2   The Components of a Decision Support System

Figure 5.2 lists several decision support tools. It should be noted that although the analytical features usually associated with DSS are not generally present in reporting and inquiry systems, they are included in this hierarchy because they are often the first type of computer support made available to marketing managers and the information they provide does support decision making. Moreover, tremendous strides have recently been made in graphical displays of data—including geographic data mapping and three-dimensional, multicolor displays—and these are greatly enhancing the decision-making value that reporting and inquiry systems hold for marketing managers.

The features Bonczek, Holsapple, and Whinston (1981) call to attention become more pronounced as we move up the hierarchy to analytical models and to executive support, group decision support, and artificial intelligence systems. At each level, the systems provide greater analytical abilities to explore why events may have occurred, to forecast what might happen under certain conditions, and to draw on diverse sorts of data, information, and experience available to the organization.

While decision support systems help marketers make decisions, they do not replace managerial judgment. Much of the utility of a DSS comes from the ability to allow a decision maker to interact with models or other forms of analysis. This interaction provides the flexibility in data analysis that is necessary because of the ad hoc nature of marketing questions and the changeable nature of marketing environments.

Hoch (1994) has developed an interesting comparison of the strengths and weaknesses of experts and decision support models. He notes that experts may have biases, be overconfident, become tired or emotional, and be inconsistent. In contrast, models are unbiased (except for specification error), are unaffected by social pressures, seek regularities, and optimally weigh evidence. Hoch also notes, however, that models know only what has been specified by the model builder, address only predetermined questions, and are rigid, whereas experts know what to ask, can provide subjective evaluations, are flexible, and have well-organized knowledge. In an ideal situation, DSS would be developed and used in ways that allow managers to combine experience and intuition with the consistent objectivity of computer-based models.

With this background information on computer-based decision support systems and the human element, let us now consider the first type of DSS, reporting and inquiry systems.

REPORTING AND INQUIRY SYSTEMS

Reporting and inquiry systems provide the marketing manager with the ability to inspect company records regarding what has occurred. At the lowest level, historical data on business activities are provided in printed forms or reports. For the purposes of effective decision support, reporting and inquiry systems also need to allow marketing managers to design their own reports and to display them quickly on a video display terminal. In this section we will look at three types of reporting and inquiry systems:

- Exception reports
- Inquiry systems
- Geographic data mapping systems

Exception Reports

An example of a low-level reporting and inquiry system is an **exception report**, in which one or more quantitative indicators of business performance are reported and compared to a "standard." The standard is typically derived from the business plan and represents a minimum expected level of performance. Where an "actual" performance indicator differs significantly from a standard, the report flags the item to alert the manager that an unexpected situation–either positive or negative—has developed.

Exception reports can be generated for any marketing program for which a performance schedule and quantitative indicators of expected achievements have been developed. For example, a new product introduction program usually includes a sales and revenue forecast and perhaps even a forecast of the number of sales outlets that will offer the product. The manager in charge of the new product may wish to review the progress of the introduction program on a daily or weekly basis and would use an exception report to do so.

Inquiry Systems

Printed reports are sometimes cumbersome and time-consuming to produce and distribute. An alternative method for reviewing historical data is through **inquiry systems**, computer-based systems that allow a manager to obtain desired information from an appropriate database whenever that information is needed. While printed reports can provide only a small amount of information, an elaborate inquiry system allows a marketing manager to access a very large variety of data on the performance of the business at any time. In addition, a well-designed inquiry system also allows great flexibility in the type of data requested and in the level of aggregation. By **level of aggregation** we mean the degree to which the data represents specific entities or events rather than a summary of many entities or events. Let's consider this concept in more detail.

LEVEL OF AGGREGATION. Ideally, marketing databases are maintained at the lowest possible level of aggregation in order to provide marketing managers with the greatest degree of flexibility. To illustrate this point, think about how an organization's sales data can be provided at different levels. At the highest level of aggregation, the data might be provided as a yearly total sales figure for all products. A lower level might break total annual sales into figures for specific products. The next level might consider specific product sales by month. A still lower level of aggregation might allow a marketing manager to inspect a specific product's sales patterns by month, regional office, and salesperson. Finally, the lowest level of aggregation, theoretically, would be represented by a single purchase event of a single identified product, for a single identified customer, at a single identified time. Once data has been aggregated to a higher level and the original data has been discarded, potentially valuable information and analytical flexibility have been lost.

The benefits of flexibility regarding the level of aggregation have been shown by Dunne and Wolk (1977), who introduced the concept of **modular component analysis**. This refers to a process of assessing the profit or revenue contribution made by product sales at each level of aggregation. For example, a product manager might observe from a high level of aggregation inquiry—that is, a general inquiry—that sales of a specific product are below expectations at the national level. To investigate this problem, the product manager would then call up on the computer a sales report by region for the product in question and observe that sales are at or above expectations in all parts of the country except the eastern region. Further inquiries would break the eastern region into specific sales offices and might reveal a specific sales office that accounts for the lower-than-expected national figure. Noting the problem, the product manager would then contact the manager of that office to begin an investigation into the reasons for poor performance of the product.

ADVANCES IN GRAPHICAL DISPLAYS. As noted earlier, advances in graphical displays have greatly enhanced the value of reporting and inquiry systems for marketing managers. Color displays with *intensity shading*—the fading of a color in or out—combined with three-dimensional designs provide a visual representation of data that goes far beyond traditional pie and bar charts. An example is Silicon Graphic's Info Navigator, which allows developers to design screen displays that provide the user with a three-dimensional map of the available data (Bylinsky, 1993). By tracing through the map, users can focus on the sections of the organization or database for which they would like information, then retrieve that information in a graphical form.

The three-dimensional approach to inquiry systems has several benefits. First, it simplifies the commands users need to know to operate the software package. It also provides great flexibility for asking diverse types of questions. In addition, the three-dimensional approach allows far more options and output information to be displayed than do traditional approaches. Most importantly, the visual image greatly improves comprehension of the meaning of complex comparisons involving several criteria simultaneously.

Geographic Data Mapping Systems

Geographic data mapping systems are a special new approach to inquiry systems, one allowing data that is coded with an address, zip code, or longitude and latitude coordinates to be located and displayed on a geographic map of the world. Using geographic data mapping systems, businesses can plot and display geographic maps that illustrate where their business activities are concentrated, where current customers are located, or where potential customers cluster (Baker and Baker, 1993; Bryan, 1993; Cooke, 1993). They can also be used to locate members of the business's distribution channel and suppliers. Specific geographic mapping applications have included market sizing, designing sales territories, business site selection, and market area analyses (Francica, 1993; Tetzell, 1993).

Industries now commonly using geographic mapping software in marketing planning and decision making include the banking industry (Tavakoli, 1993; GIS NewsLink, 1993), print media (Burkhart, 1993), insurance (Runnels, 1993), and retail sales (Lea and Direzze, 1993). In addition to private business, the development of business applications for geographic mapping systems has also been stimulated by the U.S. government's distribution of the Tiger Files (Pittman, 1990). These files are essentially mapping data sets for the entire United States that are available to the general public, including software developers who wish to build systems for plotting geographically coded data.

Inquiry Centers

Clearly, reporting and inquiry systems are an important first step in marketing decision making. By providing data on what has occurred, these systems alert marketing managers to the performance of marketing programs, positive or negative, and help pinpoint sources of exceptional performance or areas that need further detective work.

The value of reporting and inquiry systems has led companies such as General Motors to develop *inquiry centers*, special information systems offices that have the responsibility of coordinating the various data resources that might be helpful to managerial decision making. The centers also have the responsibility of developing effective systems for making data available in a way that managers will find easy to use (Barabba and Zaltman, 1992a, 1992b). For instance, PepsiCo, the company that owns Pepsi-Cola, Frito-Lay and Taco Bell, among others, has one of the most advanced systems in the world for gathering sales data from supermarkets. In addition to performing traditional data gathering functions, this system is also designed to assess trends and relay the information to executives (Rothfeder et al., 1990).

ANALYTICAL MODELS

While data on past trends of various business indicators is valuable, reporting and inquiry systems cannot by themselves identify why events occur, particularly when the event is not attributable to a specific entity, such as a product or sales office. To move to this level of decision support, we must consider analytical models.

In the context of decision support systems, a **model** is a mathematical or logical representation of a real system or part of a real system. In the case of marketing models, the "real system" is the marketing organization and its real-world marketing environment. Mathematical or logical models allow us to experiment more quickly and at less cost and risk than is possible by experimenting in the real world. Sophisticated systems for simulating test markets (STMs), for instance, have been developed to help diagnose potential product introduction problems (Clancy and Shulman, 1992). While models can be powerful tools, it is also important not to ask too much of them. In the best case, a model should be complicated enough to capture the essence of a situation but not any more complicated than is absolutely necessary.

Analytical models are computer programs that go beyond MIS reports and inquiry systems to consider *why* marketing events have occurred, to predict future events, and to select the best among several alternative marketing decisions. DSS may incorporate statistical analyses of data on past events, probability models of marketing environments and activities, and even the advice of marketing managers and experts. Sophisticated analytical models are a rapidly developing field within marketing (Dyer and Forman, 1991). Applications include sales forecasting for new products (Clancy and Shulman, 1992), product positioning (Green and Krieger, 1992), customer prospecting and market segmentation (Gilbert, 1992; Littlefield, 1992), purchasing and retail support (Lodish, 1982; Robins, 1992), and impacts of advertising and sales promotion programs (Lilien, Kotler, and Moorthy, 1992).

The ready availability of consumer purchase data from single-source and scanner systems (see Chapter 4) has also stimulated the development of marketing models. Leeflang and Wittink (1992), for example, have developed models for using scanner data to diagnose competitive reactions to new initiatives and situations. Also, Guadagni and Little (1983) have presented *logit models*—logit analysis is a type of advanced statistical technique—of consumers' brand choice behavior that use scanner data as input.

With this background, let us look at three kinds of analytical models commonly used in marketing: forecast models, simulation models, and optimization models.

Forecast Models

Forecast models use mathematical algorithms and logical propositions to interpret data in order to predict future events. Two basic forms are unconditional forecast models and conditional forecast models.

Unconditional forecast models predict future events using historical data but without explicit assumptions about environmental factors. For example, a marketing manager may wish to predict sales over the next twelve months using data on sales levels for each month in the last five years. Such models typically use statistical techniques for analyzing *time-series data*—data collected over time—regarding the frequency of a particular type of event. Unconditional forecast models typically use statistical techniques such as time-series smoothing, decomposition methods, and autocorrelation and autoregressive correlation

(Wheelwright and Makridakis, 1985). These types of statistical techniques attempt to remove unpredictable cycles and anomalies from historical data in order to reveal a basic trend that can be used to predict future events.

Conditional forecast models also use past data to predict future events, but in this type of model the assumptions about the circumstances under which the predictions are expected to hold true are explicitly built into the model. In other words, a conditional sales forecasting model would use past historical data to project future sales and might also require the manager to specify assumptions such as growth in interest rates and the national economy. A more elaborate model might build into the forecast conditions related to competitors' actions in the market. Conditional models also allow the marketer to explore alternative scenarios by trying many different values for the conditions under which the forecast is being generated. This type of model is sometimes called a *what-if model* because it allows the marketer to consider what might happen if certain events occur.

Simulation Models

While conditional models allow the marketer to simulate future events at a rudimentary level, true **simulation models** allow explicit consideration of decisions that have *probabilistic* rather than certain outcomes. This type of model explicitly recognizes the uncertainty of marketing environments and considers this uncertainty by building probability fluctuations into the predicted outcomes. Such models are sometimes referred to as *Monte Carlo simulations* because they incorporate random variation into outcome predictions. In so doing, they allow the marketing analyst to predict the likelihood of different outcomes. This allows a quantitative assessment of risk that can be used to further guide marketing decision making.

Alternative history models are a special form of simulation model in which a historical event is examined and predictions are made regarding what might have occurred under different historical conditions. Such models can be especially helpful in trying to understand how various environmental factors might have influenced a real-world outcome. The lessons learned from alternative history models can be used in decision making and to construct better simulation models for predicting future events.

Optimization Models

The third broad type of analytical model we will consider is **optimization models**, which help marketers to select the best values for inputs to marketing programs in order to maximize the achievement of marketing goals. Perhaps more than any other type of model, optimization models also help marketers to choose among several alternative courses of action in designing marketing tactics and strategy (Larreche and Srinivasan, 1981). To illustrate, a common optimization problem is how to set prices so as to maximize profitability given production costs that vary with amount of production, fluctuations in demand for a product at different price levels, and potential influences of advertising or sales promotions on demand. General Dynamics's Price Analysis System (PAS) was developed to address such real-world pricing issues (Greco and Hogue, 1990).

Optimization models can become quite elaborate in terms of the sophistication of the mathematical techniques, the statistical procedures and assumptions underlying probability estimations, the amount of data on which estimates are based, the range of influential input variables, and even the number of outcome variables to consider. If multiple outcome variables are to be considered simultaneously, a multicriteria model may be required. A *multicriteria model* considers multiple objectives and thus reflects a realistic marketing situation. Sometimes the objectives may seem to be in conflict, such as when an organization seeks to maximize both profits and market share.

Issues in Model Development

From an information systems standpoint, how can models best be developed? Although general purpose programming languages (e.g., Fortran, PL/1, Pascal, COBOL, C++, and BASIC) can be used to develop analytical models, it is usually best to take advantage of user-friendly, 4GL software. Modern general purpose statistical software packages such as SAS and SPSS and financial analysis packages such as IFPS can reduce the difficulties of developing models, accessing multiple databases, and generating text, numeric, and graphical displays (Greco and Hogue, 1990; Gray, 1988; SAS Institute, 1985).

A *DSS generator* is a special computer program that brings these capabilities together for the specific purpose of building a decision support system. Other common tools include data management software, query languages, presentation graphics generators, spreadsheets (Bedient, 1989), and linear programming systems. Some high-level spreadsheets such as Quattro Pro for Windows or Excel 5.0 also include modeling capabilities, graphics, and database interfaces that are sophisticated enough to be considered DSS generators.

The actual development of models and other forms of DSS may not be the most difficult issue marketers face, however. The bigger challenge is unifying the diverse models used by decision makers so that the models work together and can access many different databases and types of data. In some cases, outputs from one model may even serve as data for another model. On the horizon are systems that will help integrate all forms of models—even spreadsheets—and coordinate diverse databases, libraries of previously developed models, and related DSS software tools (Muhanna and Pick, 1994).

EXECUTIVE SUPPORT SYSTEMS

An **executive support system (ESS)** is a special type of DSS that combines reporting and inquiry systems with analytical modeling capabilities in a highly user-friendly format. Its purpose is to allow managers to easily review business performance indicators and explore their implications for future decisions. Although early ESS were intended to support upper-level executive decision making, today such systems are used to the benefit of managers at all levels.

The actual content of ESS varies with the needs of a business, and in many cases the data and analytical capabilities are even personalized to the needs of the executive user. For example, a hospital administrator may wish to have ready access to such key indicators as the inpatient and outpatient censuses, patient satisfaction as measured by a questionnaire, mortality rates, patient infection rates, and emergency room usage. A consumer products brand manager, on the other hand, might focus on market share, total revenue, distribution channel inventories, and changes in those figures from previous months. A manager's need to receive data at various levels of aggregation is addressed by the **drill-down capability** of many ESS. This function allows the executive to look at the details behind a number, breaking numbers down into their lower levels of aggregation as needed.

The success of an ESS may depend as much on the ease with which it can be used as on the utility of the data and decision support tools it provides. Recent research suggests that decision makers prefer simple interfaces with few options (Jiang, Curry, and Pick, 1993). This, in turn, suggests the need to carefully balance the capabilities of the system with the work styles of the executive user. While a marketing analyst may wish to have great flexibility in designing or modifying conditional and optimization models, the marketing executive may desire greater focus and may find the complexities of the analyst's system alienating and inefficient.

GROUP DECISION SUPPORT SYSTEMS

Many business decisions, including marketing decisions, are made not in isolation but, rather, in collaboration with several members of the organization. To support collaboration, group decision support systems have recently begun to be used as a supplement to individual-oriented systems (Ing, 1994; Singh, Bennavail, and Chen, 1992). A **group decision support system (GDSS)** is a computer-based system that assists with problem-solving activities involving multiple decision makers. As with ESS, GDSS integrate reporting and inquiry systems with analytical models to support decision making. GDSS also provide software to support electronic meetings and facilitate group interaction, determine group preferences, generate information from the individuals in the group, and process the information the group generates (Gray and Olfman, 1989).

The style of interaction among users of group decision support systems can vary. For example, a GDSS might keep users' contributions anonymous in order to prevent senior managers from intimidating junior staff members. This can help ensure objectivity and candor in the interactions among users as data and the output from analytical models are interpreted through group interaction. GDSS can also provide transcripts of the meetings they facilitate so that a record of the decision process is preserved.

SUMMARY

In this chapter we have introduced decision support systems (DSS) and have reviewed their basic characteristics and potential benefits. We have suggested five types of decision support systems and have reviewed four of these: reporting and inquiry systems, analytical models, executive support systems, and group decision support systems. We have also reviewed several types of analytical models, including conditional and unconditional forecast models, simulation models, and optimization models, and we have considered their applications to marketing decisions.

As we have seen, decision support systems have great potential for creating competitive advantage through better access to data and better methods of transforming the data into meaningful information to guide decision making. Keep in mind, however, that while these models improve analytical abilities, they do not make or recommend specific decisions; this requires interpretation using human intelligence.

The fifth type of DSS, artificial intelligence systems, represents an important emerging field that attempts to improve not just analytical ability but decision making itself. The exciting field of artificial intelligence and its applications in marketing is the subject of our next chapter.

Key Terms

alternative history models
analytical models
conditional forecast models
decision support system (DSS)
drill-down capability
exception report
executive support system (ESS)

forecast models
geographic data mapping systems
group decision support system (GDSS)
inquiry systems
level of aggregation

model
modular component analysis
optimization models
reporting and inquiry systems
simulation models
unconditional forecast models

Baker, S., and K. Baker (1993). *Market Mapping*. New York: McGraw-Hill.

Dyer, R. F., and E. H. Forman (1991). *An Analytic Approach to Marketing Decisions*. Englewood Cliffs, NJ: Prentice Hall.

Gray, P., and P. Olfman (1989). "The User Interface in Group Decision Support Systems." *Decision Support Systems*, Vol. 5 (June), pp. 119–138.

Lilien, G. L., Kotler, P., and K. S. Moorthy (1992). *Marketing Models*. Englewood Cliffs, NJ: Prentice Hall.

O'Brien, T. V. (1990). "Decision Support Systems." *Marketing Research* (December), pp. 51–55.

6 *Artificial Intelligence in Marketing*‡

‡ This appendix represents the joint work of Kimball P. Marshall and Roger A. Pick.

Artificial intelligence refers to the use of a computer to accomplish tasks that require a human being's intelligence when she or he performs those same tasks (Nilsson, 1980, p. 1). It is one of the most exciting growth fields in the area of information systems—first, because the very notion of intelligence is difficult to define, and second, because of the great potential for practical applications of artificial intelligence systems.

What exactly is intelligence? This question has confounded philosophers, psychologists, and biologists for centuries and certainly cannot be resolved here. For our purposes, we define **intelligence** as purposive decision-making processes that are based on consideration of relevant and available data and past experiences, carried out with the intention of achieving specified goals. **Artificial intelligence systems** are computer systems that carry out goal-oriented decision-making processes by drawing on and interpreting information derived from past experiences of human beings, data on past events, and, possibly, the experiences of the system itself. Decisions may be of a *taxonomic* nature, as when the system diagnoses a disease based on specified symptoms or when one language is translated into another. Decisions may also be in the form of recommended tactical or strategic plans. Artificial intelligence systems differ from the types of decision support systems we discussed in Chapter 5 because artificial intelligence systems incorporate inferential and deductive reasoning and heuristic manipulation of data (Chandler and Liang, 1990; Pigford and Baur, 1995; Steinberg and Plank, 1990).

In this chapter we will review two major approaches to artificial intelligence systems that have been applied to marketing decision making: expert systems (ES) and neural networks.

EXPERT SYSTEMS

Expert systems (ES) is commonly referred to as *knowledge-based systems* because they use the knowledge of experts as input information. Essentially, these software applications mimic the logic of the decision processes of human experts. ES is a mature technology in that methods for developing these systems are fairly well established and many practical applications have been created. Expert systems have been used to examine single-source data for trends, to filter marketing data for quality problems, to develop forecasting models, to set sales quotas, to qualify sales prospects, and to train sales personnel (Steinberg and Plank, 1990; Schmitz, Armstrong, and Little, 1990). In short, they are powerful tools for problem solving. Not all situations are appropriate for expert systems, however. In fact, the effective and efficient use of expert systems requires special circumstances. At least three conditions for the practical development of ES can be identified:

- The problem to be solved must be clearly defined and narrow in scope.
- There must be experts in the problem area who can express their expertise as general guidelines for decision making.
- The development of the ES should be less costly than the value of its benefits.

Let us consider these three conditions more closely. After defining the conditions under which ES can be most helpful, we will discuss several marketing-related applications of ES, then explore how they are developed.

Conditions for Applying Expert Systems

The first condition for applying expert systems is that the problem must be clearly defined and narrow in scope. Attempts to apply expert systems to broad scopes, or *domains*, of a problem generally fail. For example, an expert system might successfully solve the narrow problem of selecting an advertising medium for an ad campaign (Chadha, Mazlack, and Pick, 1991) but probably would fail if it tried to produce the actual ads. At least at this time, the development of the ads themselves would require too many ambiguous, subjective, and creative issues.

The domain of the problem may also affect the likelihood of success in an organization. The first expert systems developed by a company should be small, easily developed systems with clear, if simple, benefits. Beginning small reduces the risk of failure while the company gains experience with this kind of system. Later, as the company gains experience, expert systems may be developed that can have a significant impact on operations and competitive advantage. As is the case with any investment of a limited resource, it should be used where it will have the greatest effect.

The second condition for expert systems is that there must be experts in the problem area who can express their knowledge as general guidelines for decision making—rules of thumb—that they apply to solve problems like the one under consideration. The experts must also be articulate and willing to share their expertise because it is upon that knowledge that the ES will be based.

If the methods of solving a problem are more specific than a general rule of thumb, the problem may be more easily solved using a more conventional system. Conversely, if the expertise is less well defined than a general rule of thumb, the experts' knowledge and decision-making processes will not be able to be captured adequately and the ES will be likely to fail.

The third condition for the practical development of ES is that the development of the system should be less costly than its benefits. Because ES is expensive to develop, it should not be used if an experienced manager using the system can make decisions that are better than when the manager uses his or her own expertise in combination with more conventional DSS software.

In sum, expert systems can be most helpful for well-defined problems for which expertise is scarce yet sufficiently available and for which the benefits of the expert system make the development cost-effective. These characteristics fit marketing very well. Many tactical marketing decisions can be expressed as specific problems or objectives, and, as Mentzer and Gandhi (1992) have observed, there is a substantial codifiable body of knowledge in the marketing field upon which experts agree. Much of the knowledge that has been developed has been published. Also, costs of marketing activities can often justify the development of expert systems applications to improve decision making. This being the case, let us explore several marketing applications of expert systems.

Applications of Expert Systems in Marketing

Expert systems have been applied to a number of marketing problems, but applications in consumer packaged goods businesses have been particularly important. Consumer packaged goods marketing is a fertile context because of the rapid increase in the marketing-related data available to managers (McCann and Gallagher, 1990). It should be noted, however, that although expertise exists to analyze the data, the availability of that expertise has not increased at anywhere near the rate needed for companies to take full advantage of the new data resources.

EXPERT SYSTEMS IN BRAND MANAGEMENT. McCann (1986) has described several expert systems that have been useful to consumer packaged goods brand managers. For instance, monitoring data from single-source databases and scanner data (described in Chapter 4) may require expert systems. Because this data is less aggregated than the sales data available before scanner systems, expert systems can allow managers to shift attention, for example, from one annual national marketing plan to portfolios of regional plans that can be reassessed on a weekly basis. While this type of move from a single annual national plan to several weekly plans implies a need for more brand managers, firms are turning instead to computer-based systems for assistance, and thus becoming more competitive with fewer people.

McCann proposes a four-phase "brand management cycle," in each phase of which ES can play a significant role. These phases are (1) data exploration to identify problems and opportunities given the current market plan, (2) causal analysis to identify the sources of problems and opportunities, (3) the design of a marketing plan to solve the problems and take advantage of opportunities, and (4) implementation of the marketing plan.

During the first phase, if staffing levels do not permit conventional exploration of data, an expert system that employs rules of thumb to search scanner and single-source databases for important deviations from the current marketing plan would be helpful. Similarly, an ES with rules of thumb for finding competitive opportunities or situations requiring intervention can help brand managers by pointing out the specific parts of the marketing database that require close examination.

Help in McCann's second phase might be provided by an expert system that could construct a "best" statistical model for marketing forecasts by building a number of candidate models, comparing them, discarding some, and modifying the rest. Such a system could use rules of thumb to evaluate models and, based upon the evaluation, construct a better model. Jiang, Curry, and Pick (1993), for instance, describe a system that automatically constructed forecasting models using single-source consumer packaged goods data from a single metropolitan market.

During McCann's third phase, rules about the brand itself and the nature of the market can construct a strategy for the brand's promotion. From that strategy, a second expert system can select a specific promotion device (McCann, Tadlaoui, and Gallagher, 1990). This information might then be handed off to a more specific system to develop an advertising plan.

During the final phase, expert systems could advise the salesforce on approaches for promoting products to specific types of customers. Also during this phase, expert systems can set quotas for individual accounts, sales representatives, and marketing territories. As an example, Holsapple and Whinston (1987) have suggested a set of decision rules for a system that can plan sales quotas in the publishing business.

EXPERT SYSTEMS FOR REPORTING. Schmitz, Armstrong, and Little (1990) have described a particularly impressive system, called CoverStory, which uses several expert systems in sequence to identify important trends from scanner sales data on a product category, then automatically writes memos that summarize trends of importance to marketing managers. This system was developed by MIT, IRI, and the Ocean Spray Cranberries Cooperative and has become a commercial product offered by IRI.

CoverStory is a sophisticated *exception-reporting expert system* that constructs an English-language memorandum in three steps. In the first step, using data from the InfoScan database (Schmitz, 1994), it ranks facts about various markets and products by defined criteria. The facts ranked as most noteworthy are selected for further analysis. The second step is a search for the most important explanations for these facts. Using marketing models, the system assesses likely causal factors such as changes in distribution or price. These identified potential factors are ranked, and the most critical and likely are included in the CoverStory memo.

Finally, in the third step the system writes standardized sentences with the relevant facts inserted at appropriate locations. Memo wording is developed using randomized synonyms to keep the memos from appearing to be mechanical. A desktop publishing package then produces the output. CoverStory would be classified as an expert system because the criteria used in selecting the important facts and important causes are heuristic, although it also incorporates statistical models.

A recent extension of CoverStory is SalesPartner, which has been developed to aid consumer packaged goods sales representatives in developing presentations for fact-based selling (Schmitz, 1994). When sales representatives call on a retailer's buyer, they are generally trying to get the buyer to carry their product, put an additional version of the product on the shelf, give more or better shelf space to the product, put up special in-store displays, include the product in a store ad, or cut the shelf price for the product. SalesPartner aids the sales representative by using the retailer's own historical data in all of these areas to develop sales presentations that will show the benefits of the sales proposal.

Other marketing-related expert systems have been developed to set marketing objectives and suggest strategy options (Baugh, Gillies, and Jastrzebski, 1993), select creative advertising strategies, choose among alternative proposals for advertising copy, recommend promotion tactics, plan product portfolios, and screen new product concepts (Burke, 1994). Borch and Hartvigsen (1991) have reported on a system developed in Scandinavia to support strategic market planning by small firms. Expert systems are even being embedded in transaction processing systems (Tieperman, Inman, and Pick, 1994) to enhance customer service and therefore gain competitive advantage.

Developing Expert Systems

Developing expert systems is different from developing more traditional software. As Gallagher (1988) observes, "This is because it is not an algorithm that is being developed but knowledge that is being encoded for machine use" (p. 78). For this reason, various expert system development programs—such as VP-Expert (Pigford and Baur, 1995)—have been created to aid ES development. The expert system development process is shown in Figure 6.1. At a basic level, expert system software development requires a knowledge engineer to acquire knowledge from an expert in the problem area, also called the *application domain*. The knowledge engineer must then convert this knowledge into an expert system. This is often done using a type of software referred to as a programming shell.

KNOWLEDGE ENGINEER. A **knowledge engineer** is a computer programmer-analyst who specializes in expert system development. The engineer's job is to derive and codify the experts' knowledge as applied to the problem area. The knowledge engineer then converts the knowledge into rules to be used in the program.

KNOWLEDGE ACQUISITION. The process of gaining knowledge from the domain expert for use in the expert system is called **knowledge acquisition**. This process is often the most time-consuming portion of expert system development. The most commonly used knowledge acquisition techniques are forms of concurrent verbalization. During a **concurrent verbalization** session, the expert in the application domain is asked to verbalize his or her thoughts continuously

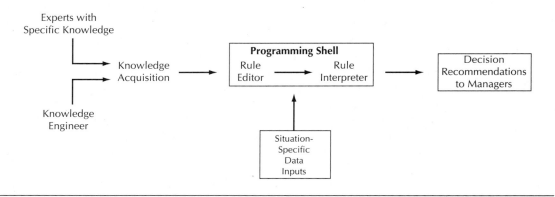

FIGURE 6.1   **The Expert System Development Process**

throughout the problem-solving process. If the expert lapses into silence, the knowledge engineer who is observing this process prompts the expert by asking, "What are you thinking about now?" or something similar. The session is audio-taped or videotaped, and the knowledge engineer takes notes. After the session, a transcript is produced from the tape for the knowledge engineer to analyze.

The idea behind concurrent verbalization is that by speaking aloud, the expert creates oral reports that reflect his or her short-term memory during the problem-solving process. Since no one can observe the expert's actual thought processes directly, concurrent verbalization converts the thought process into observable behavior. However, the technique has its problems.

First, it is stressful to both the expert and the engineer, and many experts are therefore uncomfortable with it. It is also time-consuming and tiring to both the expert and the knowledge engineer. An alternative approach, called **context focusing**, allows the expert to approach the problem as if it were a game of "twenty questions." This approach has been used successfully in a system to choose media for an advertising campaign (Chadha, Mazlack, and Pick, 1991).

PROGRAMMING SHELL.   After acquiring the expert's knowledge about the problem and the process of solving it, the knowledge engineer converts the expert's knowledge into a working expert system. This is ordinarily done using a **programming shell**, a computer program that assists in the writing and execution of the expert system. To understand the programming process, it is important to know that an expert system program is made up of a collection of *rules*, which consist of a precondition and an action. A *precondition* is something that must be true before the rule can be executed, such as "Consumer focus groups provide favorable results." The *action* tells the expert system what to do, such as "PRINT 'Launch new program.'"

The programming shell consists of a rule editor and a rule interpreter. The **rule editor** portion of the shell is a specialized text editor used to efficiently enter rules, preconditions, and actions into shell programs. The **rule interpreter**, sometimes called an **inference engine**, is a computer program that executes the shell program, searching for rules that can be executed only when the precondition is true, and then executes them according to one of several possible priority orders established by the knowledge engineer.

As impressive as the benefits and growth of expert systems applications in marketing have been, the long-term promise of new artificial intelligence technologies such as neural networks may be even greater. Although neural network systems are still in an early stage and few marketing applications have been developed, their potential makes them worth our careful consideration.

NEURAL NETWORKS

Whereas expert systems mimic experts' thinking processes, **neural networks** are computer applications that mimic the human brain. One important aspect of neural networks is their ability to learn from their own past activities in the sense that records of the system's past performance can influence processing in order to improve future performance. Theoretically, such systems could become self-improving.

Neural networks are inspired by the workings of the human nervous system. The human nervous system consists of interconnected cells, called *neurons*. When the input signals to a neuron exceed a threshold, it sends a signal through its output. This output, in turn, becomes input to other neurons. The idea behind computer neural networks is that flexible, adaptable computer systems can be developed by simulating the learning-by-experience processes of the human brain. This is done by constructing software neurons—or *controlled pathways*— that pass signals to each other.

Much of the excitement about neural networks arises from the fact that they simulate not only the brain's reasoning but also its learning capabilities. Imagine an intelligent software assistant that trains itself! Since our brains are estimated to have about 10 billion neurons with 100 trillion interconnections, we are obviously a long way from being able to simulate the human brain. Nonetheless, this approach to artificial intelligence has generated much recent enthusiasm and experimentation (Proctor, 1992; Mentzer and Gandhi, 1992).

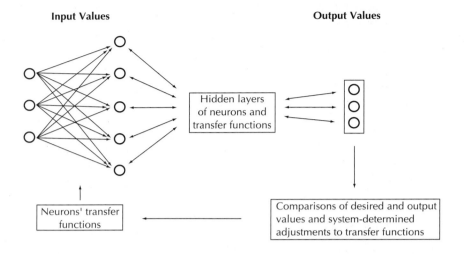

FIGURE 6.2   The Neural Network Trial-and-Error Learning Process

Using Neural Networks

As shown in Figure 6.2, a neural network is organized into a layer of input neurons, a layer of output neurons, and one or more hidden layers that interconnect the input and output elements. Each data input to the network corresponds to a single simple variable, such as a given week's sales, price, or advertising level. These data inputs are provided to specific input neurons. Each neuron assesses the data it has received and then sends a signal to other neurons. This process is repeated through the layers of neurons as the "logic" process is carried out, until output data is computed by an output neuron. As data is received, each neuron computes a value (or a set of values) based on its inputs. The computed values determine the data signals the neuron sends and the neurons to which it directs its signal. The method of carrying out these calculations and defining and directing the next signal is the neuron's *internal transfer function*.

As a learning system, a neural network is trained by giving it a set of inputs and desired outputs. The neural network then computes outputs of its own, compares them to the desired outputs, and, if necessary, adjusts its transfer functions to reduce the difference between the resulting outputs and the desired outputs. Then the neural network compares the outputs again. This trial-and-error "learning" process continues, sometimes for a long time, until the desired outputs are achieved.

The main limitations of neural networks are that (1) the process must begin with a set of inputs that serve as indicators of the conditions under which the decisions are to be made and (2) indicators of the outputs that are desired. The input training data set must be complete enough to train the network on most types of circumstances likely to arise (Zahedi, 1993). Ideally, the training data set is developed from real-world historical conditions and known outcomes, is relatively large, has few errors, and is divisible into a training set and a testing set. The *training set* is used to "train" the system, and the *testing set* is used to compare the results of the trained system with what actually occurred. This allows the developer to assess how well the neural network can predict outcomes of input conditions. The better it can predict real-world outcomes under specified conditions, the better it can recommend courses of action to the user.

Applications of Neural Networks in Marketing

As we noted earlier, neural network applications in marketing are in an early stage of development. One marketing application where neural networks are already useful is in sales forecasting, given various environmental conditions and marketing actions and expenditures. Forecasting sales data is particularly appropriate to neural network applications because we have a wealth of historical data from which to develop the training and testing data sets. Additionally, because statistical methods are also used for sales forecasts, comparisons can be made between neural network systems' accuracy and that of statistical forecasts. These comparisons have found that neural networks outperform simple statistical forecasts but not sophisticated multivariate time-series techniques (Chang and Jiang, 1993a, 1993b).

Although other neural network applications in marketing are limited at this time, researchers have documented several interesting applications. Kestelyn (1992) has studied how neural networks can be used to identify the "best" sales prospects for a telemarketing operation to call from a list of customers who have not been active recently. Westland (1992) has presented systems that save busy executives time by identifying and organizing environmental and internal information for them. Also, Proctor (1992) has observed in an intriguing report the potential of neural networks for evaluating new product opportunities.

Developing Neural Networks

Like the systems themselves, much of the development of neural networks still operates today through trial and error. While at present there are no firm rules or guidelines for designing these systems, a recognizable development process has begun to emerge (Zahedi, 1993). The chief requirements for developing a neural network are data and a neural network simulation tool. As we noted earlier, the data is used to train and test the neural network.

After defining the problem in specific terms, the first step in developing a neural network is to specify the architecture of the network. This involves deciding how many hidden layers will be between the input and the output layers, as well as the overall topology of their interconnections. It is usually not clear in advance how to answer these questions, and the developer will probably have to experiment. Software development programs called **neural simulators** allow the developer to specify learning rules that will be used by the individual neurons to adapt their transfer functions. As with the questions about the architecture, these rules may need to be modified after observing the system.

After the network has been designed in terms of the number of input and output neurons, the number of hidden layers, the interconnections among the neurons, and the rules each neuron will use to adjust its transfer function, the training data set can be applied to the new system. Once training is complete, the utility of the system can be assessed using the testing data set. If testing shows that the system is accurate and robust enough to be useful in a wide variety of situations, the neural network can be put into practical operation.

SUMMARY

In this chapter we explored the role of artificial intelligence in marketing by reviewing expert systems and neural networks, how they can benefit marketing managers, and the processes by which they are developed. Although expert systems development is quite time-consuming, expert systems have made—and will continue to make—important contributions to marketing management through applications ranging from product and advertising planning to automated approaches to data analysis and environmental scanning.

Neural networks, although still in an early stage of development, also have great potential. As learning systems, neural networks do not depend on expert experience or theories to develop accurate predictions of outcomes that may result from specified situations. The ability to develop accurate predictions without experts or theoretical guidelines may mean that neural networks will be able to be applied to an even wider range of decisions or problem areas than expert systems. In a changing world, experience and theory are sometimes in scarce supply and their utility may be uncertain. Moreover, the growing abundance of data produced by our information-oriented society is likely to provide more opportunities to experiment with artificial intelligence systems and to develop more and more practical applications.

At this point in this book, we have reviewed the opportunities for competitive advantage that MKIS can offer, reviewed the many types of internal and external data resources on which these systems can depend, and considered a wide range of decision support tools that can help marketing managers make good use of their available data resources. Now it is time to turn our attention to the organization itself and consider the processes of planning, developing, and implementing a comprehensive marketing information system.

Key Terms

artificial intelligence
artificial intelligence systems
concurrent verbalization
context focusing
expert systems (ES)

inference engine
intelligence
knowledge acquisition
knowledge engineer
neural networks

neural simulators
programming shell
rule interpreter
rule editor

READINGS FOR MORE INFORMATION ON TOPICS IN CHAPTER 6

Gallagher, J. P. (1988). *Knowledge Systems for Business: Integrating Expert Systems and MIS*. Englewood Cliffs, NJ: Prentice Hall.

McCann, J. M., and J. P. Gallagher (1990). *Expert Systems for Scanner Data Environments: The Marketing Workbench Laboratory Experience*. Boston: Kluwer Academic Publishers.

Mentzer, J. T., and N. Gandhi (1992). "Expert Systems in Marketing: Guidelines for Development." *Journal of the Academy of Marketing Sciences*, Vol. 20 (Winter), pp. 71–80.

Tieperman, J., R. A. Inman, and R. A. Pick (1994). "Expert Systems: A Service Industry Exigency." *Industrial Management and Data Systems*, Vol. 94, No. 1, pp. 9–12.

Zahedi, F. (1993). *Intelligent Systems for Business: Expert Systems with Neural Networks*. Belmont, CA: Wadsworth.

Creating a Marketing Information System

7 Planning a Marketing Information System

In previous chapters of this book, we reviewed the components of marketing information systems and how a MKIS can contribute to attaining a competitive advantage. We also reviewed data resources that firms can access and decision support tools that marketing managers can use to transform data into information for decision making. We now turn our attention to the process of creating a MKIS. This process has three broad stages: planning, technical development, and implementation. As experienced system developers can attest, however, these stages are not a simple linear progression of steps. Rather, knowledge and experience gained in the technical development stage can lead to a reevaluation of the MKIS plan. Experiences gained in implementation can lead to still more changes. To help you understand these processes, this chapter introduces each stage and then considers the specific steps of the planning stage in some detail. Chapters 8 and 9 then address the specific steps involved in the MKIS technical development and implementation stages.

AN OVERVIEW OF THE MKIS CREATION PROCESS

Recall from Chapter 1 that a MKIS is a comprehensive, ongoing system, not just a quick solution to a short-term problem. Indeed, as a "formal and ongoing system" intended to guide marketing decision making, the MKIS will require careful planning and coordinated development. While this is true of most formal information systems projects, a MKIS provides special challenges. One important way in which a MKIS differs from many other types of information systems projects is that the questions and data needs of marketing managers often occur on an ad hoc basis (Greco and Hogue, 1990). In other words, because marketers operate as a boundary department, adapting the organization to its uncertain and changing external environments, their information needs and the approaches they use to analyze this information often change. The information system to support marketers must therefore be flexible and yet still provide for data and analytical integrity.

The challenge of MKIS development is further complicated by marketing managers' use of desktop computer systems and user-friendly program packages to carry out their own programming activities. Microcomputers and easy-to-use data analysis programs such as Lotus 1-2-3, SPSS, SAS, and many others have given marketers the ability to develop their own reports and approaches to data analysis. Such end-user capabilities can provide workers and managers with flexibility in carrying out their jobs. However, while end-user programming can be an asset to the information systems specialist and to the organization, it must be managed and planned if all users are to have access to the data they require and if the organization is to be confident in the results of the users' analyses.

The creation of a MKIS is also complicated by the need for security and centralized data administration. Security is needed because much of the data on which marketers depend is proprietary and confidential to the organization. Centralized data administration is needed because the data used by marketers might originate in, or be used by, other departments. It is important, therefore, that MKIS data be freely provided to marketing managers but also that it not be inappropriately distributed or its content changed.

To meet these special challenges while at the same time providing marketing managers with the best opportunities possible to benefit from the myriad available data resources and decision support tools requires formal, well-organized efforts. The three-stage approach to creating a MKIS—*planning, technical development, and implementation*—provides a framework for organizing this complex process. These are logical stages for any systems development project. However, to accommodate the nature of marketing activities, several writers have suggested specific activities. Cox and Goode (1967), for example, suggested seven steps for the MKIS development process, and Marshall and Lamotte (1992) elaborated these steps and adapted them to more current computing environments. Here, we organize the process around the three main phases and, drawing on this previous work, suggest a series of steps for each phase. The three stages and their respective steps are summarized in Figure 7.1.

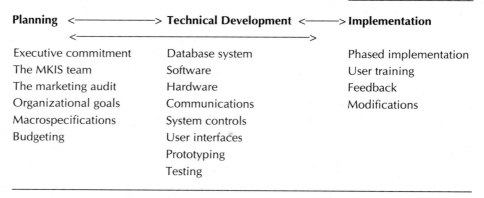

FIGURE 7.1   A Model of the MKIS Creation Process

Note that the arrows in Figure 7.1 go in two directions. This is to remind you that the process is really very interactive. As knowledge and experience are gained in later stages, the MKIS developer may have to return to an earlier stage and modify plans or even whole systems. To some people, this process may seem inefficient. Managers might ask, "Why can't the work be done right the first time?" It is not that the work is not done right; it is that information systems, and particularly marketing information systems, are tools to enhance the effectiveness of human beings who have *changing* needs and ways of working. Therefore, while we will present the stages and steps for creating a MKIS in a logical sequence, bear in mind that flexibility is the key to developing a dynamic system that will best meet the needs of the organization and its marketing managers. Let us now briefly review each stage of the MKIS creation process.

Planning

Planning is a process that has the goal of either (1) establishing the environment and guidelines for effective development and implementation of a MKIS or (2) abandoning the MKIS creation effort at an early stage if it is found not to be feasible in light of the organization's resources and priorities. The steps in the planning stage allow the organization to decide whether or not to commit to the MKIS effort and, if so, to specify the capabilities of the system, allocate resources for its development, and define the time frame in which the project will be completed. This approach may go beyond what some people think of as planning. It includes efforts to prepare the organization for a major commitment of time, financial resources, and people, and it involves the development of expectations that can be achieved (Cox and Goode, 1967; Marshall and Lamotte, 1992). It is only after the organization has been prepared with realistic expectations that what is more traditionally thought of as the planning process—such as budgeting and resource allocation—can begin.

Technical Development

The **technical development** stage of the MKIS creation process is the stage in which actual programming is accomplished and the fundamental system is established (see Figure 7.1). The MKIS database must be begun in this stage, and software and hardware must be selected. A communications system must be developed so that the MKIS will be available to users where they work and so that the appropriate data resources will be available to the appropriate software. System controls must be developed to govern access to the system and to maintain its integrity. **System integrity** refers to the ability of the system to function as expected and to provide accurate data and analytical techniques. User interfaces must be established, and prototypes of the system must be constructed. **Prototypes** are preliminary "mock-ups" of the system that have limited or no real functions. Prototypes are shown to the user for feedback. Finally, system modules must be tested as they are developed. In **testing**, actual system components are made available to selected marketing managers. After a system module is tested and approved, it can be implemented and made available to all intended users.

Implementation

Implementation is the last stage of the MKIS creation process as outlined in Figure 7.1. But remember, there is no final stage per se. If the MKIS is successful, it will be an ongoing system that changes as the requirements of marketing managers and the technologies of information systems change. Indeed, flexibility is a fundamental aspect of a MKIS. Furthermore, as is probably clear to you at this point, the MKIS is a very complex system composed of a large number of subsystems and capabilities. In fact, it is unrealistic to think of a MKIS as just one system that will be installed or implemented at a given point in time. Instead, specific components of the MKIS may be installed as they become available. This is called **phased implementation**, and it involves installing, providing documentation for, and making available to users one part of the MKIS at a time. Through phased implementation, the organization can benefit from each component of the MKIS as it becomes available rather than waiting until all components are developed.

As each component of the MKIS is implemented, the MKIS development team will be concerned with developing effective approaches to user training and procedures by which users can provide feedback for modifications that will make the system more helpful to marketing managers. **User training** refers to the processes by which persons who are intended to use the system are provided with instruction. User training may involve developing user-friendly documentation, holding training classes, and even providing personal instruction. The members of the MKIS team can often help to initiate new users. During training activities, as well as later, the users and the MKIS team will discover potential ways of improving the system. Methods of capturing feedback—users' assessments and suggestions—should be developed, as should procedures for evaluating and implementing valuable suggestions. If a decision is made to modify the system, it will be necessary to return to the planning stage to develop specifications for the modification and to budget the necessary resources.

At this point, we have broadly reviewed the three stages of the MKIS creation process. Now let us return to the planning stage to consider the specific steps in this stage that will prepare the way for the technical development and implementation phases.

THE MKIS PLANNING PROCESS

A marketing information system begins with planning. Recall that planning is a process that has the goal of either (1) establishing the environment and guidelines for effective development and implementation of a MKIS or (2) abandoning the MKIS creation effort at an early stage if it is found not to be feasible in light of the organization's resources and priorities. Substantial commitments of human and financial resources are required for any major information systems effort to succeed and benefit an organization, and substantial cooperation is needed from all areas of the organization. This is all the more true for a marketing information system, since a MKIS will draw on information resources generated by departments throughout the organization and will involve managerial decisions that influence the core aspects of the business. For these reasons, the MKIS planning stage must involve six steps:

- Securing executive commitment
- Establishing the MKIS team
- Executing a marketing audit
- Developing organizational goals
- Defining macrospecifications
- Budgeting

As depicted in Figure 7.2, the planning stage involves both traditional planning activities and the preparation of the organization for the two MKIS creation stages that follow—technical development and implementation. Both of these activities are tied to the planning stage because effective planning must be carried out with the organization's goals and commitments in mind. Without this, the system to be developed could not effectively aid decision making. In the following sections, we will review each of the six steps of the planning stage to develop a clear understanding of what must be accomplished in each step in order to achieve a successful MKIS.

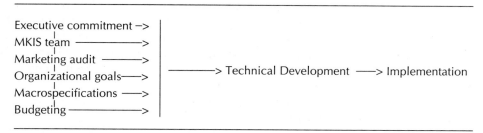

FIGURE 7.2   The Steps of the MKIS Planning Stage

Securing Executive Commitment

The first major step in the MKIS planning process calls for obtaining a clear commitment of support from top management. There are several reasons why top management support is needed early in the planning process. The first is to allay the inevitable politics of human organizations. Creating a MKIS requires access to data from many departments in the organization. It requires the cooperation of department managers and executives, each of whom may have different priorities.

Some department managers may see the MKIS as a good idea but may also believe it is "marketing's problem," not theirs. Other managers might feel threatened if they are asked to release information related to their own department's activities. For example, sales and marketing departments are separate in some organizations. Data on sales by salesperson, sales office, and sales territory will be of interest to marketing managers and will need to be included in a MKIS. A sales manager might feel, however, that releasing this information might not be to his or her advantage, because it could lead to changes in commission plans or in ways the salesforce is managed. If such political problems are to be avoided, a mandate from the organization's senior executives must be provided to validate the planning effort and to avoid time-consuming roadblocks (Keen, 1981). Some managers might continue to grumble, but top management will have made their expectations clear.

A second reason for obtaining early high-level executive commitment is that the MKIS effort will be expensive, in terms of both people and money. Assigning people to a MKIS planning and development team requires that they be released from other assignments, which, in turn, requires that priorities be established. The urgency of the MKIS effort must be balanced against other demands senior management might wish to place—or may already have placed—on the information systems (IS) department and the marketing department.

It is not sufficient for top management to simply authorize persons interested in MKIS to proceed. On the contrary, if a serious MKIS effort is to be made, top management must understand the current demands placed on the IS and marketing departments and be prepared to forgo other initiatives. Similarly, money is a scarce resource that must be allocated by top management. Although the exact costs of the development effort may not yet have been estimated, top management must consider whether the MKIS project will be of sufficient importance to make it a financial priority. If not, it will be difficult to gain support for the necessary expenditures later, when they occur.

Obtaining top management support requires that the proponents of a MKIS in the IS and marketing departments work together to develop the vision of how the MKIS can create competitive advantage by enhancing decision making. This cooperative effort requires the proponents to consider the organization's culture and beliefs regarding the types of information relevant to good business decisions, the ways in which information is used in decision making, and the value of environmental scanning and analysis (Daft and Lengel, 1986; Daft and Weick, 1984; Hambrick, 1982). In addition to helping obtain executive support, creating a vision of the potential benefits also helps the MKIS proponents gain cooperation from other sections of the organization and avoids undue concerns among marketing personnel in the marketing audit step.

A clear show of commitment from top management should include an organization-wide announcement of the initiation of the MKIS planning effort. The communication should convey the vision of how a MKIS will benefit the organization. It should also assign responsibility for carrying out the marketing audit to the MKIS proponents and the director of marketing. By including the director of marketing on the audit team, top management may reduce anxiety among members of the marketing department.

Top executives also need to inform all managers of their obligation to support the effort; however, until a final decision to proceed with the MKIS development is made, the mandate from top management is limited to proceeding with the marketing audit. The findings of the marketing audit will provide a clearer perspective of how MKIS tools can enhance marketing decision making. At that point, top management can form the MKIS team, whose members will proceed with the remaining steps of the planning process.

Establishing the MKIS Team

The second step in the MKIS planning stage is the formal appointment of the MKIS team, the group that will lead the remainder of the planning effort as well as the technical development and implementation stages. This step requires careful selection of a team leader and of team members.

THE TEAM LEADER. The team should be led by a high-level manager to ensure cooperation throughout the organization and effective communication with all senior executives. This person should have the confidence of top management and a clear understanding of the organization's marketing activities and strategic goals. These are more important qualifications than expertise in information systems. The political and resource issues the team will face require a leader who can communicate the MKIS project's value to other executives and the organization's personnel. Therefore, the team leader should not be a middle manager from a technical area or one with limited experience in the organization. Instead, the team should be led by an executive who can serve as the project champion.

TEAM MEMBERS. Other members of the team should be drawn from the information systems and marketing departments, because members of these departments will be involved in the development process and will also be the users of the MKIS. Representatives from the marketing department should be selected for their broad experience in all of the firm's marketing functional areas so that they will be sensitive to the needs of all marketing personnel. Team members should also have the confidence of the members of their own departments because the team members will be the liaison between the team and their departments and will later have the responsibility of explaining the benefits of the MKIS and how it can be used.

Teamwork between the information systems staff and the marketing staff must be emphasized, beginning with the formation of the team. Members from each department must understand one another's needs, vocabularies, and functions within the organization so that they will be able to work together well. If effective working relationships have not developed in past projects, or if a history of difficulties exists, the team leader may wish to consider the use of outside consultants to help overcome "us-versus-them" attitudes.

Managers from all departments must recognize that involvement on the MKIS team is a primary responsibility of team members and that workloads must be adjusted accordingly. Whenever a team is formed to address a "special project," there is a risk that team members will suffer from "role overload" because they will also be expected to complete their usual full-time responsibilities as well as their new assignment. If workloads are not adjusted to allow for the realistic time requirements of the MKIS effort, team members may be forced to neglect the MKIS effort while meeting their department managers' demands. The result will be failure of the MKIS effort. Therefore, the team leader needs to be in a position to monitor team members' work responsibilities, be part of each team member's evaluation process, and have easy communication with the superiors of all team members.

Executing a Marketing Audit

The marketing audit represents the third step in the MKIS planning stage. The objective in this step is to develop a clear understanding of the marketing issues facing the company. The marketing audit also makes known the data resources and decision procedures used by the marketing managers. This audit should include the perspectives of top-level managers so that their data requirements and decision procedures can be incorporated into an assessment of how MKIS technology might improve marketing decision making. While marketing audits are often carried out by external consulting firms to ensure objectivity (Kotler, Gregor, and Rogers, 1977), it is possible for the firm to use high-level marketing managers such as the director of marketing to supervise the audit. Whether or not the organization decides to use an external consultant, marketing managers and IS personnel must be involved in the audit because the findings will be used to guide the establishment of organizational goals, macrospecifications, and budgets for the MKIS. **Macrospecifications** are the broad definitions of the intended users' system requirements (Marshall and LaMotte, 1992).

Traditionally, marketing audits have been carried out with the intention of improving the firm's overall marketing performance. Kotler, Gregor, and Rogers

(1977), in their article "The Marketing Audit Comes of Age," define a **marketing audit** as

> a comprehensive, systematic, independent, and periodic examination of a company's—or business unit's—marketing environment, objectives, strategies, and activities with a view of determining problem areas and opportunities and recommending a plan of action to improve the company's marketing performance. (p.25)

The marketing audit should focus on assessment of six aspects of the company's marketing situation (Kotler, Gregor and Rogers, 1977):

- Environmental analysis
- Marketing strategies
- Marketing organization
- Marketing systems
- Marketing productivity
- Marketing functions

ENVIRONMENTAL ANALYSIS. The environmental analysis, as we defined it in Chapter 2, should include a review of the overall industry in which the company operates and the more immediate environment composed of the company and its customers, business partners, and direct competitors (Kotler, 1991). This environmental analysis can sensitize the MKIS planners to the external information needs of marketing managers as well as help developers and managers anticipate new information needs that may arise in the future.

MARKETING STRATEGIES. The environmental analysis leads to reassessment of the current marketing strategies to determine whether these are consistent with the opportunities and threats discovered in the environment. The **marketing strategies audit** reviews decisions and plans regarding in which markets to participate and with which products, philosophies for differentiating the company and its products from competitors and their products, and objectives that focus on exploiting strengths and overcoming weaknesses. In addition to providing the marketing department with the opportunity to reassess its marketing objectives, the strategy audit also gives the MKIS planners an opportunity to explore how MKIS technology might be applied to achieving those objectives.

MARKETING ORGANIZATION. The **marketing organization audit** focuses on the current effectiveness of the marketing department and related departments (such as sales), as well as the effectiveness of working relationships between marketing and other divisions. For example, a successful marketing program requires coordination with sales activities, production, inventory handling, purchasing, quality control, distribution, engineering, and research and development. By reviewing current relationships between marketing and other departments, MKIS planners can identify the internal data that is needed for effective marketing management and can identify points of organizational stress that might be alleviated through better information flows.

MARKETING SYSTEMS. Not only must marketing coordinate with other departments, marketing managers must also continually evaluate, monitor, and control their own programs. The **marketing systems audit** allows for the assessment of procedures for such activities as sales forecasting, establishing sales goals and quotas, physical distribution, product development, product elimination, and determining advertising effectiveness. Auditing of these systems should include identifying the data used to monitor and control them, the reporting techniques that are in place, and the management guidelines for determining success. Information from these audits will suggest data requirements for the MKIS as well as the types of decision support systems that would improve control of marketing programs.

MARKETING PRODUCTIVITY. The marketing productivity audit and the marketing functions audit that follows it are similar to the systems audit. The **marketing productivity audit** focuses on the costs of marketing activities and seeks justification for expenditures. This audit is often particularly problematic for marketing organizations, because the benefits of marketing activities are often indirect and removed in time from the activities themselves (e.g., the benefit of a national television advertisement may be increased sales sometime later). This makes it difficult to measure productivity. If the audit reveals specific concerns, however, a MKIS planner can include ways to capture helpful data and statistical modeling tools for assessing productivity impacts of marketing expenditures.

MARKETING FUNCTIONS. **Marketing functions audits** are detailed reviews of specific functional areas—such as advertising, pricing, sales, and product management—that the systems or productivity audits indicate have serious problems. By focusing on known problem areas, MKIS planners may be able to identify applications that can produce direct benefits for the organization. Focusing on known problems may also help to clarify the vision of MKIS benefits and strengthen top management support.

Developing Organizational Goals

For the MKIS team's efforts to be successful, it is important that the MKIS team determine the organization's needs, establish realistic goals and expectations regarding the MKIS, and then communicate these to the rest of the members of the organization. This step is important because information systems change the sociotechnical context of work; such changes sometimes result in anxiety over job security and job change (Woodward, 1965). By establishing and communicating goals, the MKIS team allows personnel to see what changes may take place and to know that their employment status is secure. At the same time, the goals and expectations must be realistic and not be aggrandized in order to generate resources or top management support. Unrealistic expectations will lead to disappointment among users when the MKIS is implemented and may even impede the system's development by preventing decision makers from agreeing on its limitations.

DETERMINING NEEDS. The findings of the marketing audit are the starting point for determining needs and developing goals. Goals and expectations should focus on improving the information flows and decision-making processes studied in the marketing audit. It is often useful to focus on certain marketing areas—such as sales management, pricing, promotional programs, and product management—in order to identify specific needs or opportunities. For example, the marketing audit might have shown problems in designing sales territories or in monitoring salesperson performance. The audit of the decision processes by which prices and channel margins are established might have revealed the need to improve information flows and decision support for these processes. Some companies may have difficulty evaluating advertising and other promotional programs. This may lead to the development of systems that monitor advertising programs and assess their impact. Product management is a particularly important area for consideration. Goals may need to be established to improve product managers' access to relevant product sales and market share information, or to improve their abilities to identify specific product performance problems.

ESTABLISHING GOALS. The specific opportunities for improved use of information systems that were identified in the marketing audit should be addressed as organizational goals. In doing so, two considerations must be kept in mind. First, the goals must be described in terms that emphasize how the proposed systems can *help* marketing managers, not replace or de-skill their jobs. It is important to have the support of all marketing managers throughout the development process; therefore, it is important for the goals to reflect their needs and be relevant to the problems they perceive in their roles.

Second, the organizational goals must be realistic. Any tendency to enhance the MKIS project by creating unrealistic expectations or by endorsing a manager's "wish list" simply to gain support must be avoided. Goals must be stated in terms of practical, realistically achievable enhancements to the information and decision support needs of marketing managers and top managers. Goals and expectations should emphasize realistic time frames, personnel time, and financial resources.

Realistic time frames should be stressed because organizations often operate with a short-term view. To facilitate setting realistic time frames, it will be useful to develop a series of specific goals that address discrete marketing activities. This way, the MKIS development can be carried out in a modular fashion, allowing priority to be given to certain activities. This will allow the organization to experience early practical successes with the MKIS project as the high-priority modules become available. This will also help to avoid delays due to the development of less critical parts of the system. For example, a decision support system to facilitate pricing activities might be suggested as a first achievement if it can be accomplished relatively quickly. A comprehensive system for monitoring advertising effectiveness, on the other hand, might be treated as a separate activity to be developed over a longer period. Even this might be broken into smaller projects that could be developed sequentially, with each system providing needed marketing decision support as it comes on-line.

OBTAINING MANAGEMENT COMMITMENT. Once the organizational goals are established, the MKIS team presents them to senior management for review, approval, and prioritization. This step allows senior executives to reiterate their commitment and clarify their vision of the MKIS. It also allows top management to raise concerns early in the process, perhaps avoiding the possibility of wasted efforts later. For instance, if senior managers do not understand certain goals or do not perceive them to be relevant, these goals can be reassessed or restated.

Finally, by presenting goals with time estimates and anticipated resource requirements to top managers, the MKIS team is verifying that the resources are available and committing itself to the proposed goals and time frames. If top management adjusts the goals or cannot support the anticipated resource requirements, the MKIS team will have to revise expectations. Once top management accepts the goals and supports the anticipated resource requirements, the team can begin the development of macrospecifications, which will be followed by formal budgeting.

Defining Macrospecifications

The process of defining macrospecifications builds on the MKIS goals by specifying the systems needed to achieve these goals. For each given goal, the macrospecifications address

- the specific capabilities the system will provide;
- the types of data on which it will draw;
- the types of decision support tools required;
- the general nature of the user interfaces; and
- the types of hardware needed.

For example, if one of the goals is to develop a system for monitoring salesperson performance, the macrospecifications might call for access to salesperson commission records, product sales records, and shipping records and for database management software to integrate these databases (Collins, 1985; Steinberg and

Plank, 1987; Wolfe, 1990). The macrospecifications might also call for spread-sheet or statistical software to summarize and analyze the data and for geodemo-graphic software to display the information on visual maps that can be easily understood by top management. Finally, the specifications would include the hardware, including output devices, required for running the system (Cooke, 1993). This level of specificity is needed both for realistic budgeting in the next step of the planning process and for the technical development stage to proceed smoothly. Thus, the development of macrospecifications is vital to the rest of the MKIS project.

DEVELOPING SPECIFICATIONS. To ensure accurate macrospecifications, the MKIS design team must carefully study the computer systems currently used by marketing, as well as new "state-of-the-art" approaches to marketing decision support. It is also important to review the marketing audit and carry out additional interviews or focus groups with marketing managers in order to better understand their decision-making processes (Keen, 1981; Mayros and Dolan, 1988; Nylen, 1990). Managers' personalized approaches to information selection, analysis, and decision making must be considered because the MKIS is intended to support these managers.

Marketing managers must also have trust and confidence in the underlying processes of the support systems that are developed. The more the MKIS team involves marketing managers in the development process, the more likely are marketing managers to trust its development. MKIS developers may find it help-ful to describe and graphically illustrate their understanding of the marketing managers' decision support processes so that all parties can verify that the techni-cal descriptions reflect how decisions are actually made. With these understand-ings confirmed, the MKIS team can propose and test commercially available software or develop software in-house.

MODULAR PLANNING. The development of accurate macrospecifications will reveal the full complexity of the MKIS project and may in some cases expose a project so large that its continuation is questioned. In these instances, it is useful to consider a *modular approach* for organizing MKIS macrospecifications. A modular approach makes the project more manageable; it also allows the MKIS team and top managers to prioritize development of the specific modules that are proposed. Such an approach must include a plan to integrate the modules into a comprehensive system when development is complete. Also, because the various marketing functions are integral parts of the overall marketing program, different MKIS functional modules will probably share common data needs. For this rea-son, the MKIS macrospecifications should include a central marketing database system on which all modules may draw.

WRITTEN DOCUMENTATION. The result of the macrospecifications step is a written document that serves as a technical development and evaluation guide for the overall system and for each proposed module. The specifications must be integrated into one document that sets clear goals for the technical developers. Written documentation is necessary too as a reference to resolve disagreements and to ensure logical interfaces throughout the system. Periodically, as macrospecifications change over the life of the system, the written documentation can be adjusted to reflect new requirements.

Budgeting

The budgeting process involves accurately estimating the hardware, software, personnel, consulting, and related needs of the technical development and implementation stages. Historically, budget estimates for information systems projects have been grossly underestimated, and cost overruns and time delays remain common (Laudon and Laudon, 1988). For this reason, careful specification of hardware requirements over a fixed period of time should be developed from macrospecifications. The MKIS team should also review the MKIS software requirements and obtain preliminary bids for commercially available software. This will make cost estimates more accurate and may help the MKIS team make cost-saving decisions.

The budgeting process should also include a proposal for how the MKIS project will be formally housed in the organization. This includes specific descriptions of full- and part-time staff and managerial positions, reporting lines, signature authorities, and miscellaneous support costs (e.g., office supplies). These organizational plans should distinguish between a temporary organization for the development and implementation stage and a permanent arrangement for staffing, funding, and managing support for the system after it is in use.

Upon completion, the budget should be presented to top management for review and approval. This step provides an additional opportunity for executive-level recommendations and further extends top management's commitment to the project. By allocating and assigning responsibility for resources—human, financial, time, and physical—as well as delineating reporting lines, worker evaluations, and signature authorities for purchases, the organization creates a formal office from which the MKIS technical development stage can be launched. Without this formalization of the project, the MKIS effort would be only an ad hoc attempt to apply technology to marketing decision making and would be doomed to failure due to role conflict and overload among the programmers and support personnel, constant delays for basic expenditures, and reassignment of staff priorities.

SUMMARY

The development of a marketing information system is a complex process that requires substantial planning and resources. However, like most complex activities, the development of a MKIS is manageable if it can be broken down into stages and steps and if each step is carefully carried out. In this chapter we have briefly reviewed each of the major stages of creating a MKIS—planning, technical development, and implementation—and we have reviewed in detail the specific steps of the planning phase of creating a marketing information system.

The steps of the planning stage move the organization from a vague sense that technology can enhance the cost-effectiveness of marketing functions and create competitive advantage to a formal, organized effort for specific achievements. The planning stage begins with executive commitment and the formal establishment of a MKIS team. Next comes a marketing audit, from which proponents of the MKIS create a vision of the system. Based on these goals, macrospecifications that establish the technical requirements of the system are defined. These macrospecifications guide not only the technical development and implementation stages of the MKIS project but also the budgeting process by which resources are allocated and responsibilities assigned. In all steps, top management is informed and input is sought. Once the MKIS development team is established as a formal office in the organization, the technical development stage can begin.

Key Terms

macrospecifications	marketing strategies audit	system integrity
marketing audit	marketing systems audit	technical development
marketing functions audits	phased implementation	testing
marketing organization audit	planning	user training
marketing productivity audit	prototypes	

READINGS FOR MORE INFORMATION ON TOPICS IN CHAPTER 7

Boynton, A. C., and R. W. Zmud (1984). "An Assessment of Critical Success Factors." *Sloan Management Review* (Summer), pp. 17–27.

Buttery, E. A., and E. M. Buttery (1991). "Design of Marketing Information Systems: Useful Paradigms." *European Journal of Marketing*, Vol. 25, No. 1, pp. 26–39.

Daft, R. L., and K. E. Weick (1986). "Toward a Model of Organizations as Interpretation Systems." *Academy of Management Review*, Vol. 9, No. 2, pp. 284–295.

Dunne, P. M., and H. I. Wolk (1977). "Marketing Cost Analysis: A Modularized Contribution Approach." *Journal of Marketing* (July), pp. 83–94.

Kotler, P., W. Gregor, and W. Rogers (1977). "The Marketing Audit Comes of Age." *Sloan Management Review* (Winter), pp. 25–43.

Krcmar, H. A. O., and H. C. Lucas, Jr. (1991). "Success Factors for Strategic Information Systems." *Information and Management*, Vol. 21, No. 3 (October), pp. 137–145

8

The MKIS Technical Development Stage

After consensus has been reached among marketers, top management, and the MKIS team regarding the goals, macrospecifications, budgets, and staffing, the MKIS creation process enters the technical development stage. In this stage, the MKIS goals and macrospecifications are transformed into computer systems with applications programs that access and analyze the required marketing data. To achieve this, a large number of complex issues must be considered. As shown in Figure 8.1, these development issues are

- creating the MKIS database system;
- defining decision support software requirements;
- defining hardware requirements;
- developing a communications network;
- developing systems controls;
- designing user interfaces;
- constructing prototypes of system components and their operations; and
- testing system modules.

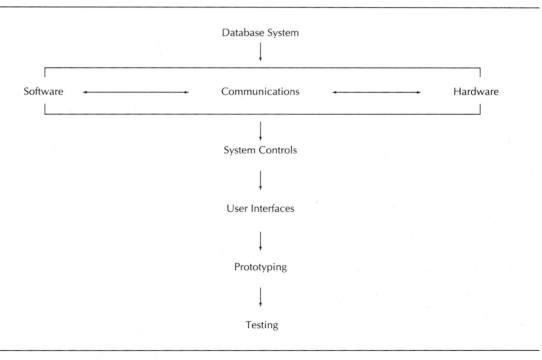

FIGURE 8.1   Steps in the MKIS Technical Development Stage

Like planning, technical development is an interactive process, not a linear one. As such, developments proceed with progress in each area influencing the development of related systems in other areas. However, as suggested by Figure 8.1, we can present the steps of technical development in a logical sequence in order to better explain each one. Because the heart of the system will be the MKIS database, we begin this chapter by considering the database as the first step in the technical development phase. We then address each of the remaining technical development tasks in the order presented in Figure 8.1 so as to offer you a comprehensive review of the development process. Readers who are not yet familiar with database concepts may wish to review the Appendix for a short introduction to the language of databases.

CREATING THE MKIS DATABASE

We referred to the MKIS database as the heart of the MKIS because it provides the data that will guide marketing decision making. Remember that the MKIS has two basic goals: (1) to maintain an ongoing flow of relevant data and (2) to provide a means for analyzing data and reporting information in a manner that can guide marketing decision making. The purpose of the database system is to achieve the first goal. Effective development of the database system will allow applications software development to focus on analysis and reporting with confidence that the data that will feed MKIS applications is accurate and available in the expected locations and formats.

Four tasks underlie the development of the database system:

- Development of a data dictionary
- Development of data files and the procedures by which data is entered into the MKIS
- Development of data integrity and access controls
- Designation of a database administrator

Let us look at each of these steps in more detail.

Developing a Data Dictionary

Just as the database system is the heart of the MKIS, the data dictionary is the heart of the database system. A **data dictionary** is a formal document that identifies all data items and files that will be used by the MKIS and integrates these into a common database system. Under the task of developing the data dictionary, we include (1) identification of the relevant data items needed for MKIS applications, (2) identification of sources of these data items, (3) specification of data files that will contain these data items, and (4) documentation of the source, location, and meaning of each data item within a file.

The data dictionary must be a comprehensive, written document because it will guide further programming of the MKIS applications. At the same time, however, it should also be viewed as a "living" document, just as the MKIS itself is a living system. To understand this, consider that if the MKIS is developed in a modular fashion with high-priority applications being addressed first, as we recommend, the data dictionary will initially document only the data used by those applications. When new data items are needed, they can be added to existing data files, or placed in new data files, and documented in the data dictionary. If, over time, certain data items or files are found not to be needed any longer, these can be deleted from the database system and from the data dictionary.

The first step in developing any application is to identify exactly what data needs to be input to the application and the specific sources of the data. The macrospecifications that were developed in the planning stage guide the MKIS developer in making these decisions. In earlier chapters of this book, we reviewed a wide variety of data sources. Recall that data may be derived from ongoing internal business operations systems or from external data sources that may be either on-line or off-line. If the external data sources are on-line, the organization's computer systems may be able to link to the external system on a regular basis and electronically transfer—or *download*—data into the organization's system, where the data can be stored in a file for future access by the MKIS. Off-line external data may be provided on diskette, on computer tape, or even in the form of hardcopy records that must be entered into the computer system by hand.

Whatever the source, the data dictionary must document the required data items, their source, the form in which they are available, and the procedures by which they are to be entered into the MKIS database. This documentation will then be used to direct the task of developing data files and the procedures by which data will be added to the MKIS system.

Developing Data Files

The tasks of developing data files and devising procedures for entering data into the MKIS involves transforming the data dictionary documentation into actual data files in the system. At this stage, the MKIS development team may be working on the organization's central computer system or on a *satellite system*—a smaller system linked to the main system. If the team is working on a satellite system, the developers must have access to files on the central system. This is necessary so that they can develop procedures either for creating MKIS data files to feed the applications under development or for allowing the applications to have direct access to data files that are routinely maintained by the internal operations systems used in ongoing business operations, such as order entry, shipping, inventory, and customer satisfaction systems.

Judgments must also be made regarding whether an application should have direct access to an operations system file or whether software should be created to abstract data from an operations system file and store it in a MKIS-specific file. In cases where an operations system routinely updates its own record system—the likely scenario—developers may be able to insert an output module into the operations system to write out a new data file that will be used by the MKIS. In this way, the MKIS file can be routinely updated as a part of the ongoing activities of the operations system and the MKIS user will not have to directly access a file used by the business operations systems. This procedure is desirable because it protects the integrity of both systems.

Procedures for building MKIS data files using external data may be more cumbersome. Difficulties sometimes arise in communications between sources and also with variations in how data is coded and defined by different sources. If a close working relationship exists between the organization and the external source, MKIS developers may be able to work with the external system's administrator to arrange an automated procedure for downloading data and updating MKIS files in the desired format. On the other hand, if external sources will not allow automated transfers, the external source may have to supply a computer tape or diskette containing the required data in a standard format on a regular basis. In this case, the MKIS developers can write administrative procedures for receiving data, registering the data, and then transferring the data to the appropriate MKIS file in the appropriate format.

All of these procedures must be carefully followed and must also be documented in the data dictionary. Data obtained from occasional or ad hoc market research projects can be handled in a similar way. Formal documentation must be maintained in all cases, however, so there will be no confusion regarding the meaning, quality, or timeliness of the data. Such confusion would inevitably waste MKIS developers' time, undermine user confidence in the MKIS system, and lead to erroneous management decisions.

At this point, it is also important to think about how MKIS data files can be developed as relational databases (Marshall and Lamotte, 1992; Cox and Goode, 1967). Whenever possible, data should be maintained at the lowest practical level of aggregation and common designations for date, time, product types, salespeople, geographic locations, customers, business partners, and so forth should be used (Curry, 1993). This method allows data in different files to be linked and also allows MKIS users flexibility in developing analytical approaches.

In the past, system administrators may have preferred hierarchical file structures because these can save disk space and computer time. While hierarchical structures might be acceptable if the system's goals are fixed reporting and tree-style searches for individual records, they too greatly constrain the analytical capabilities required by marketers. Therefore, low levels of aggregation and relational database structures are best for addressing the flexibility needed by marketers.

Developing Data Integrity and Access Controls

The third task in the development of the MKIS database system addresses data integrity and access controls. These controls are part of the broader issue of systems controls but are noted here because specific attention should be given at this point to three issues:

- How to protect proprietary data in the MKIS from unauthorized access
- How to ensure that data items will not be changed inadvertently by a user of an applications program
- How to protect the system from the risk of electronic viruses that might be transmitted into the organization's computer systems from external data sources

To help with these issues, the MKIS developers may be able to take advantage of the security features of the hardware platform's central operating system to determine which user accounts will be allowed access to which data files. This limits the risk of data being accessed by persons who might download proprietary information for inappropriate reasons. The operating system's control subsystem may also be able to maintain logs of accounts that have accessed certain files and what activities were carried out on these accounts.

Additionally, the operating system's security controls may be able to limit access to files so that most accounts can read data from a file but cannot write on it. In this case, the "privilege" of writing on a file is limited to the system administrator who updates files. Finally, system controls already in place to protect the central system from viruses (disruptive computer programs planted by someone trying to sabotage a computer system) may also be applicable to the MKIS system. Virus detection and cleaning should be included as part of the daily maintenance of the system.

Designating a Database Administrator

To ensure the integrity of the MKIS data system, a MKIS database administrator position must be formally created. A knowledgeable person in the information systems (IS) department is the best candidate to fulfill the job responsibilities of this position. The administrator's responsibilities should include

- maintaining the data dictionary in hardcopy and on-line forms;
- directly carrying out or supervising all file updating activities, such as maintaining the necessary links between MKIS applications and data provided by

internal operations systems and external systems, adding new data to the MKIS database, and pruning unnecessary data from it; and

■ maintaining MKIS data integrity and security.

The database administrator job should be viewed as a permanent position in the organization and should be staffed and budgeted as a part of the IS long-term operating budget. To ensure responsiveness to marketing department needs, a high-level marketing manager should be included in the personnel evaluation process for the database administrator.

DEFINING SOFTWARE REQUIREMENTS

Like the MKIS database requirements, the MKIS software requirements are derived from the macrospecifications document. By **software requirements**, we mean the specific decision support software that will provide marketing managers with the analytical and reporting capabilities described in the macrospecifications document. Various types of decision support systems (DSS) tools were reviewed earlier in this book. It should be clear from that discussion that the particular decision support software required depends on the organization and its specific needs. Three issues must be considered regarding the decision support software needs of the marketing managers:

■ What specific applications are required by marketing managers and how these are prioritized

■ Whether software should be developed in-house or purchased from commercial vendors

■ What ongoing software documentation and technical support will be required

Selecting Specific Applications

As with database management, we recommend a modular approach to software development. Following the priorities identified in the macrospecifications document, MKIS developers can focus on specific applications that can be brought on-line quickly and provide substantial benefits to the organization. While many marketing decisions are interdependent, analyses related to specific marketing functions are often carried out separately, and many decision support applications can therefore be developed as discrete system resources following the guidelines of the macrospecifications document.

The macrospecifications document not only suggests decision support needs but it also indicates the specific logical processes followed in marketing decision making. These processes, which are derived from the marketing audit, provide direction regarding the required analytical capabilities of the software. In some instances, the analytical requirements will be unique, in which case in-house software may need to be developed. This is true, for example, with expert systems in which the decision-making rules are specific to the organization (Chandler and Liang, 1990). In many cases, however, the analytical requirements of marketing managers will be more generalizable, making exploration of commercially available software feasible. Examples of these requirements include multivariate statistical modeling, econometric forecasting, and geodemographic mapping.

Development Options and Technical Support

Commercially available software offers several advantages over software developed in-house. First, commercial software can often be installed and modified to meet a specific application more quickly than an in-house program can be created. Also, because commercial software may be used by many organizations, it is usually more fully tested than a new program developed within the organization. Finally, a commercial software license may include technical support provided by the vendor. These benefits can substantially speed MKIS development and help to keep the project within budget. On the other hand, commercial software may have a number of disadvantages. It may be expensive, including both initial charges and periodic licensing fees. In addition, commercial software sometimes restricts the number of users who can simultaneously access the software. Last, there is the possibility that commercial software packages might not be available for the organization's particular hardware.

Where commercial software is affordable, is appropriate to the available hardware, is well tested, and meets the application requirements, MKIS developers should give strong consideration to its use. Software developed in-house may appear on the surface to be less expensive, but considering the real number of personnel hours involved in programming, testing, refining, documenting, and maintaining the system, the lower cost may be an illusion.

One valuable option for MKIS developers to consider is the purchase of commercially available, generalizable program packages that combine the benefits of commercial and in-house software. These packages, such as SAS, SPSS, and IFPS, serve as platforms that can be customized to meet individual users' needs. They often combine a wide range of statistical, simulation-modeling, graphics, and report-writing capabilities with efficient database management software. Powerful packaged systems can also allow MKIS developers to create customized applications for a wide variety of marketing functions relatively quickly. Moreover, the fourth-generation language (4GL) programming techniques of these packages often allow MKIS users to build personalized applications that draw directly on the MKIS database system. This added flexibility can save considerable technical support time over the life of the system and can greatly enhance the benefit of the MKIS to a knowledgeable user.

Selecting commercially available software can be an uncertain process. Among the steps developers can take to simplify the process are compiling lists of potential suppliers by asking marketing managers about software commonly used by colleagues in other organizations, reviewing advertisements in marketing trade publications such as *Marketing News*, and hiring outside consultants. Potential suppliers should be investigated by contacting their users for information on such issues as the utility of the software for the types of applications in question, the vendor's responsiveness to problems, and the quality of technical support. Special attention should be paid to each software package's hardware requirements and the ability of the software to draw on the MKIS database system.

DEFINING HARDWARE REQUIREMENTS

For the MKIS software to operate effectively, the appropriate hardware must be provided. Therefore, the hardware requirements should be considered simultaneously with the development of the software. Developers need to address at least three issues:

- Hardware configuration for software compatibility
- Standardization of marketing workstations
- Allocation of hardware resources

Hardware Configuration

Hardware configuration issues may be classified into three types: CPU decisions, data storage requirements, and input/output requirements. First, let us look at the types of decisions that need to be made regarding the CPUs.

CPU DECISIONS. The term **CPU**, or **central processing unit**, is used here to refer to the microprocessors that carry out the computational and logical work of the computer system and related electronic memory devices and interfaces to other equipment. Early in the development process, the MKIS team must determine the types of CPUs to which specific applications will be assigned. Related to this is the decision regarding which type of overall computer system will be used.

Three broad types of computer systems are (1) a *central system*; (2) a *fully distributed processing system*, in which each user has her or his own CPU but draws on the centralized databases; and (3) a *mixed system*. In the mixed system, users carry out some applications on networked desktop computers, and these, in turn, are linked to more powerful computers that serve as network hubs. The hubs can run other applications and provide users with access to a larger-scale central system for still other applications. After the type of system and compatible CPU configurations have been determined, software selected to support MKIS applications can be assigned to the appropriate CPU.

While all three types of systems have their advantages, a mixed system should be most carefully considered because it can take advantage of both the excellent fourth-generation languages and user-friendly software of the desktop systems and the CPU-intensive, large database applications appropriate to midrange distributed systems or large mainframe systems. A mixed system also simplifies coordination of the databases because they can reside on a central system accessible by authorized users via their distributed CPUs. On the other hand, a mixed system does have its disadvantages. First, it might complicate data access and intersystem communications if the central system does not run the same operating system as the distributed CPUs. Also, it may be difficult to develop simple approaches for users to switch from one system to another.

DATA STORAGE REQUIREMENTS. Once the base CPU system has been defined for a specific MKIS application, developers can decide what the configuration of the CPU itself will be. Sufficient internal random access memory (RAM) must be provided to meet the requirements of the software that will be assigned to the CPU. Careful estimates of the on-line disk storage requirements of the software and the MKIS data must then be made. For instance, large databases may require extensive central system disk storage capabilities. Storage devices that will hold data downloaded from the central database may also have to be added to distributed CPUs. Even software designed for desktop systems may require large-capacity hard disks and CD-ROM capabilities to support the software or special external databases. For example, extensive databases are provided on CD-ROM by the U.S. Census Bureau. Some geographic mapping systems and scanner data vendors also provide their data files on CD-ROM disks. In fact, CD-ROM drives are now so common that they should be considered a standard piece of any new system.

INPUT/OUTPUT DEVICES. Decisions regarding the appropriate input/output devices are governed by the requirements of the software chosen to support marketing applications, as well as user needs and organizational budgets. DSS software designed for desktop systems is often graphics-intensive and requires SVGA color graphics monitors. Other software applications may require high-quality hardcopy output devices, such as thermal color printers and high-resolution laser printers.

Standardization of Workstations

Users' needs must also be taken into account when making workstation decisions. Developers must consider whether standardized workstations should be developed for all users of the MKIS. **Standardized workstations** are desktop computer systems configured in the same way for all users. One advantage of standardized workstations is that technical support for the MKIS is simplified. Also, common user interfaces can be used for many applications, thus simplifying user training. Finally, there may be cost savings associated with purchasing equipment in quantity. Users requiring applications that need more capability than the standard workstation can access a distributed midrange CPU or the central mainframe. Basic output devices can be supplied as a part of the standard workstation. More expensive output devices, such as high-resolution color printers, can be made available and shared by users through a distributed network.

Allocation of Hardware Resources

Organizational budgets affect hardware resource allocation decisions. Resource allocation decisions are greatly simplified if a distributed computing network with standardized workstations is implemented. Even so, it is necessary to determine which marketing managers and staff members will be assigned their own workstations, which staffers will share a workstation, and which sections of the organization will need high-quality output devices. In principle, these decisions should be based on the nature of the MKIS applications used by the different members of the marketing department and the resources required by those applications; however, internal political considerations often have strong influence on allocation systems. Moreover, equipment allocation decisions made at this stage of the project will largely be constrained by the needs that were anticipated in the budgeting step of the planning stage. If the budget was realistically designed, even new needs resulting from software considerations during the technical development stage should not result in serious surprises regarding hardware.

DEVELOPING A COMMUNICATIONS NETWORK

As you can probably tell from our discussion, a MKIS may involve many software applications. These applications may operate on different types of computer systems, but they are all linked by access to a common database system. Such a complex system presents a variety of communications challenges, several of which we will discuss here.

Common Challenges in Developing a Communications Network

First, developers need to create a system in which each workstation can have access to the central database system when authorized MKIS users need access to the MKIS data. This requires MKIS developers to establish communications links between each workstation and each CPU on which MKIS data or applications are located. In the language of networking, such links may be referred to as **point-to-point communications**.

Second, because marketing is an organizational process, users will need to electronically share the results of MKIS applications with other users. Accordingly, MKIS developers need to establish an electronic-mail system through which documents and other output from the applications programs can be transmitted to other MKIS users and to any members of the organization who are not regular MKIS users.

A third communications challenge is how to govern the electronic traffic in the MKIS system. At any given time, two or more users of the MKIS system may attempt to access the same MKIS data file or applications program. Therefore, communication protocols that will govern system traffic must be established. These may involve setting priorities for certain types of users and for certain types of applications, as well as defining system procedures.

Selecting a Networking System

Careful selection of an effective networking system addresses most of the communications issues that challenge MKIS developers. Such a system should be able to coordinate access to network file server CPUs that, in turn, allow access to data and software located on the network. To network the same types of workstations (e.g., a personal computer network), developers may use well-tested networking software from a number of commercial vendors. Common protocols include IBM's token ring networking approach and Novell's baseband Ethernet. Such networking software typically includes administrative control options to govern an account's access time, privileges related to reading and writing files, and the ability to access other workstations on the system. Also, such software often includes electronic-mail options.

The situation is somewhat more complicated when different types of computers must be linked into a common network. This type of situation arises in a mixed distributed processing system that involves, for example, a central IBM mainframe serving as the repository of most of the MKIS data files, a series of VAX systems providing special application software, and MS-DOS personal computer systems running DOS and Windows applications. In this case, MKIS developers need to use some form of bridge software to link these diverse systems. Fortunately, commercial vendors have developed a variety of approaches to solving such communication problems and it is unlikely that original programming will be needed. Even with commercial software, however, substantial time is required for designing, installing, and administering the communications system.

Because communications systems can be highly complex, this field requires special expertise. Developers should consider using expert consultants in designing the communications system, selecting communication software and hardware vendors, and installing the system. This expertise may be needed again as new MKIS applications modules and data files are brought on-line.

DEVELOPING SYSTEMS CONTROLS

As noted in the discussion on database systems, developing systems controls requires significant attention. **Systems controls** are enforceable rules designed to protect data integrity and security, govern access to the system, and coordinate users' activities. We can classify systems controls into two types: software systems controls and organizational procedural controls.

Software Systems Controls

Software systems controls are administrative capabilities provided by the operating system software, the communications system software, or specific applications software. They allow a system programmer to create new accounts for persons wishing to use the system, define privileges for each account on the system, set system priorities for accounts and types of activities, and otherwise govern access to system resources.

Organizational Procedural Controls

Organizational procedural controls are written rules and policies established by the organization for maintaining data integrity and system security and for coordinating usage of the system. Organizational procedural controls govern, for example, how new data is entered into the system and how old data is deleted, as well as how a user can apply for an account. They also provide guidelines for establishing the privileges and priorities that are assigned to an account, the decision processes by which new software requests are evaluated, and so forth. While many of these policies are included in the macrospecifications document, formal procedures continue to evolve throughout all stages of technical development and implementation, and over the life of the system.

System Administrator

A member of the MKIS technical support staff should be assigned the responsibility of serving as the system administrator. The **system administrator** has access to an account that has the highest level of privileges, and he or she can set privileges for all other accounts. The system administrator's responsibilities include establishing accounts and their privileges, setting priorities for sharing CPU time and data resources among simultaneously operating software applications and related user demands, and coordinating users' activities with those activities of the MKIS technical support staff in order to ensure compliance with organizational procedural controls. Therefore, to effectively maintain secure operations of the system, the system administrator must have both software management and office management responsibilities.

DESIGNING USER INTERFACES

Even after the appropriate data has been made available and the appropriate applications software, communications systems, and system controls have been developed to support the work of marketing managers, the system will not succeed if marketing managers do not feel comfortable using it. One of the strongest determinants of marketing managers' satisfaction with a MKIS is the user interface. User interfaces, you may recall, include the video displays, audio displays, and hardcopy printouts by which the system communicates with the user, as well as the keyboard commands and other processes by which the user enters commands into the system.

Historically, the interfaces between computers and their users have been very technical and required substantial knowledge of cryptic commands composed of special words, called *syntax*, in order to perform meaningful operations. These systems are called "user-hostile." Today, high-speed computers with high-level graphics capabilities have greatly improved the "friendliness" of computer systems by using fourth-generation languages and graphical menus of commands. In these user-friendly systems, commands can be selected by using cursor control keys to highlight and select options or by using a mouse to move an arrow on the video screen to select options. As the user moves the mouse, its movement is translated to changes in the location of the arrow on the screen. When the arrow is located on a specific option, that option may be selected by pressing a button. Options are often represented by graphic pictures called *icons*. The appearance of the icon is supposed to suggest the nature of the command.

In designing effective user interfaces, the MKIS developer must consider issues such as

- the tasks that will be required by the users;
- the data inputs that may be required by a user of an application;
- the options related to the analytical tasks;
- the layout of the results of an application program's operations on the screen and on paper;

- the user's current computer tools; and
- individual factors such as computer knowledge, computer phobia, and user's status among coworkers.

MKIS developers should be especially sensitive to the "sociotechnical" situation of MKIS users (Davis and Olson, 1985; Triste and Lawrence, 1963; Mumford and Wier, 1979; Hackman and Oldham, 1980; Woodward, 1965). For example, user-friendly interfaces that require only low levels of computer literacy will enhance the system's acceptance, while complex interfaces that require time to master and risk making a manager appear inadequate are likely to be rejected. To avoid problems and user resistance, developers should actively involve users in the design of the interfaces. It will be particularly important to have a well-designed help system on-line, as well as support personnel, to educate users and help them solve problems.

Where possible, MKIS developers should attempt to develop interface procedures that resemble computer operations with which the users are already familiar. Even if this is not possible, the users' current computer activities should be studied for ideas. Ideally, the new MKIS applications should be seen as enhancing current procedures, not imposing new processes. User support documentation should explain new MKIS procedures in the language of the users' earlier applications.

Finally, by involving users in the design of user interfaces, developers can enhance user acceptance of the MKIS. When users are involved in designing the style of the interfaces, they can give developers feedback regarding user interfaces and make recommendations for improvements. This leads to more user-friendly interfaces and will provide the users with a sense of involvement and ownership that will lead to more ready acceptance when the system or its modules are actually made available. Prototyping, the next stage of the MKIS technical development process, offers an excellent opportunity for effective user involvement.

CONSTRUCTING PROTOTYPES

As defined in Chapter 7, prototyping is the process of creating a preliminary model of an anticipated system so that it can be presented to users for evaluation. The prototype might be a "microversion" of the real system or a nonfunctioning shell that only simulates the system. In either case, it should include realistic user interfaces including video screens; data, analytical, and output options; and simulated output. The MKIS team can save considerable time and expense by presenting prototypes of MKIS modules to users early in the development process. With early user feedback, costly misunderstandings can be discovered and corrected before substantial programming has occurred. User feedback may also suggest that new options are needed or that other suggested options are not needed.

It is especially useful to present prototypes to focus groups of potential users so that users may share their experiences and ideas with one another. **Focus groups** are collections of several persons—typically, eight to ten—who are asked to address a specific topic in a group interview. The benefit of a focus group, as opposed to individual interviews, is that in the group interview situation, the group members share ideas. This sharing of ideas often stimulates new ideas that might otherwise have been overlooked (Stewart and Shamdasani, 1990).

Whether obtained through individual interviews or in focus groups, the feedback gained from presenting prototypes to users can be included in the development of the MKIS modules. Periodically throughout the development process, especially as improvements are made, the MKIS team should continue to present the module's interfaces and characteristics to users for ongoing guidance. Users who provide such guidance may become proponents of the system and can be used to test the system as the full module is brought on-line.

TESTING SYSTEM MODULES

The final stage of the development of a MKIS module is testing. Testing, in which actual system components are made available to selected marketing managers for their feedback, must go on throughout the programming process in order to verify that the data can be correctly accessed and that calculations and other forms of analytical processing and reporting are correctly carried out. A testing phase should also be included after the full module is developed and installed on the actual computer system the MKIS users will use. At this stage, selected users are asked to test the system with "real-world" applications and then to compare the results to those derived from the decision-making approaches they used in the past. Additionally, users should be asked to verify that the module meets the requirements laid out in the macrospecifications document and that it accurately meets the decision support needs of marketing managers.

If each step of the development process has been carefully carried out and user feedback during prototyping has been implemented, the testing stage should produce few surprises. As each module is installed, selected users should be asked to use the new module and report any errors, or *bugs*, they find, as well as any characteristics of the system they find frustrating or dissatisfying. Users can also make valuable suggestions for ways to improve the MKIS. The MKIS developers need to assess user feedback carefully and be prepared to modify modules to improve satisfaction.

Finally, users should be asked to review the documentation and training programs as they are developed for each module. Users may offer recommendations for simplifying and improving the documentation and training plan. With this feedback, the MKIS team can make the needed modifications before making the module available to all marketing managers who wish to use it. At this point, the MKIS creation process can move to the implementation stage.

SUMMARY

This chapter has reviewed the steps of the technical development stage of the MKIS creation process. This stage involves the design of the MKIS database system and appropriate applications software required to support marketing decision making. This stage also requires that MKIS developers identify the hardware on which the system will operate and design a communications system by which users can both access the needed software and data sets and share the results of MKIS applications with one another. Developers must also carefully consider a variety of systems controls—in the form of software controls and formal organizational procedures—that govern the operations of the system, protect data integrity, and coordinate authorized user access to the MKIS.

As the system is developed, guidance is sought from users in the design of user interfaces, because these most directly affect users' experiences and satisfaction with the system. To ensure that the MKIS modules accurately meet the needs of the marketing mangers, prototypes are created and presented to groups of users beginning early in the development of each module. In this way, potential problems can be identified and avoided before substantial investments have been made in programming time, hardware, or software. When each module is fully developed, it should be tested by selected marketing users who can compare the results of the module with previous approaches to addressing similar problems. These users can also review the documentation and training programs designed to support the module and can suggest system modifications before the module is released to all users. When a MKIS application module is ready to be released, the implementation stage of the development process can begin.

Key Terms

central processing unit (CPU)	organizational procedural controls	software systems controls
data dictionary		standardized workstations
focus groups	point-to-point communications	system administrator
	software requirements	systems controls

Chandler, J. S., and T. P. Liang (1990). *Developing Expert Systems for Business Applications*. Columbus, OH: Merrill.

Davis, G. B., and M. H. Olson (1985). *Management Information Systems: Conceptual Foundations, Structure, and Development*. New York: McGraw-Hill.

Lucas, H. C. (1986). *Information Systems Concepts for Management* (3rd ed.). New York: McGraw-Hill.

Mayros, V., and D. J. Dolan (1988). "Hefting the Data Load: How to Design the MKIS That Works for You." *Business Marketing*, (March). pp. 47–69.

Stewart, D. W., and P. N. Shamdasani (1990). *Focus Groups: Theory and Practice*. Newbury Park, CA: Sage.

9 *The MKIS Implementation Stage*

If the planning and technical development stages of the MKIS creation process have been successfully carried out, then marketing managers and senior managers are well prepared for the implementation stage and it should proceed smoothly. Successful implementation of a MKIS requires that four activities be carried out under the direction of the MKIS administrator. As indicated in Figure 9.1, the four implementation activities are

■ phased implementation;

■ user training;

■ feedback; and

■ modifications.

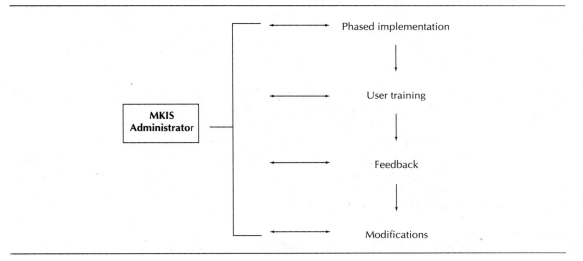

FIGURE 9.1   **Activities in the MKIS Implementation Stage**

The implementation stage is a continuous, logical process in which new modules are developed and old modules are modified or removed to adapt the MKIS to new information opportunities and changing organizational needs. In this chapter we will discuss each of the four implementation activities and how they contribute to the ongoing success of the MKIS, which, in turn, contributes to competitive advantage for the organization.

Despite the best preparation of the organization, the process of actually implementing modules of the MKIS can cause anxiety among workers and disruption to the organization. The MKIS team must be aware of the organization's level of acceptance as modules are made available and must carefully balance between initiating too much change too quickly and providing too few analytical tools to satisfy expectations. To achieve this balance, a phased implementation approach will be helpful. Recall from Chapter 7 that phased implementation involves installing, providing documentation for, and making available to users one part of the MKIS at a time. If an older system is already in place, phased implementation might involve **phased conversion**, in which one system is gradually replaced by another. This latter approach has the advantage of allowing users to become used to the new system before removing the old one. Ideally, both systems would operate at the same time so that the new MKIS is seen as enhancing opportunities, rather than disrupting current work. Eventually, however, the older and less functional system is removed and the new system takes its place.

Where a modular approach to MKIS development has been used, the phased implementation process can proceed even while other MKIS modules are in development. This is because each module can be brought on-line and made available as it completes its own technical development stage, so long as it does not depend upon another module that is not yet available. Key elements of the MKIS, however, such as the basic database system, hardware workstations, a communications system, and system controls, must be in place before analytical modules are implemented, since the analytical modules must draw on these essential elements to function.

Benefits of Phased Implementation

Phased implementation has three benefits. First, it allows the organization to experience the support of the MKIS modules as soon as they are available. With appropriate prioritization of modules, the most important components of the MKIS can be developed and implemented first. This strategy allows marketing managers to begin benefiting from the MKIS long before the entire system is on-line.

The second benefit is that users can adapt to the MKIS one step at a time. This may reduce users' anxiety levels and resistance to the new tools. Technological systems change how work is carried out, and workers often experience anxiety about changes in the work environment. Even where every effort has been made to involve users in the planning and development process, some anxiety and resistance should be expected, because users need to learn new approaches in order to take advantage of the MKIS.

The third benefit of phased implementation is workload management. As MKIS modules are brought on-line, demands are placed on the MKIS programmers for user support, training, and adjustments of the system as bugs are inevitably discovered. By phasing in modules one at a time, demands on both users and programmers can be kept manageable.

Installation

During phased implementation, the hardware for workstations, networked computers, and other resources is acquired, installed, and tested. The hardware and wiring needed for the communications system are also installed in this stage. With the physical infrastructure in place, the next step is to install the software selected or developed for the MKIS on the appropriate computers. This includes software related to the operating, control, communications, and database management systems. At this point, the system can be tested.

After system controls are established and user accounts are created, the marketing department members of the MKIS team can test the communications system by using electronic mail and by linking each workstation to all other networked computers (to the extent that the appropriate system privileges allow). With the ability to easily connect to any required computer, users can also test the inquiry capabilities of the database system. If the basic hardware and software infrastructure of the MKIS is successfully installed, attention can turn to installing the first MKIS analytical module, which can then be tested by the MKIS team.

Documentation

As each module is installed, documentation for both the users and the system administrator must be developed. This documentation supplements the data dictionary created in the technical development stage and provides the base for user training. User documentation should be *task-oriented*, because the intended users of the documentation are marketing managers, not information systems specialists. Examples of specific user tasks include how to sign on to the system, how to use electronic mail, how to attach to other computers used by the MKIS, and how to carry out simple inquiries using the MKIS database system.

As additional MKIS modules for decision support applications beyond basic inquiries become available, they are installed on the system by the system administrator. In turn, appropriate documentation must be developed for each module as it is installed and tested and before it is released for general use. User-oriented documentation of analytical modules should include an explanation of the task objective of the module, descriptions of user interface screens and commands, descriptions of analytical options, and examples of actual applications. With this documentation in place, the implementation stage can shift to user training.

Recall that user training is a systematic approach to providing users with written documentation, on-line documentation, a help system, and peer support as each component of the MKIS is implemented. The objective of user training is to educate users on how to use the MKIS modules efficiently in order to achieve their inquiry or analysis goals. The incorporation of practical applications into user training will help lead to greater acceptance of the module and speed its use in actual work for the organization. The training must be considered unsuccessful if users complete the training but do not use the module in their work. If problems are found in the module during the training process, the experiences gained in the training activities can be used as information to guide modifications of the system.

Task-oriented Documentation

User training requires task-oriented documentation and trainers who are familiar with both the MKIS and marketing activities. **Task-oriented documentation** is written instructions designed for the user of the system and organized around the specific tasks that must be performed to achieve the system's objectives. Therefore, both the user's decision processes and the system's logical organization of steps must be considered as this documentation is developed. Task-oriented documentation is different from the documentation used by the systems analyst or programmer in that it is concerned with how to use the system to achieve a specific end-user goal. Systems analysts and programmers, on the other hand, are more concerned with why the system works and how the system functions technically.

To illustrate task-oriented documentation, let us imagine that a user wants to take advantage of an expert system for pricing that uses monthly sales of a current product as input to suggest optimal prices for a new product. The user will have to perform a series of tasks. First, the user needs to sign on to the system by using her or his password. Second, the user must activate the expert system by using a specific command. Once the expert system is activated, the user is presented with a set of options for how to proceed. Instructions for signing on and activating the system, along with explanations for each option, must be included in the documentation. Next, the user is required to select a data file and, from it, to abstract monthly sales information on a given product. Again, task-oriented documentation must explain how this should be done. Parameters and choices that can be entered when exercising each option must also be explained in connection with that option.

Trainers

The best trainers are often MKIS team members who come from the marketing department and the marketers who tested the system during the technical development stage. As trainers, they not only introduce the new MKIS module and its benefits to their peers but, as respected colleagues, they may also be able to serve as opinion leaders. This is particularly true if they are seen actively using the system with clearly visible, practical results.

Task-oriented documentation and the appropriate trainers are also important for training senior-level managers, who may require special approaches to training, for at least two reasons. First, top managers may be more impatient than department staff because greater demands are placed on their time. Because MKIS training may at first seem like a distraction from pressing duties, it is useful to apply, if possible, the MKIS module to a current problem faced by the manager so as to help the manager feel that his or her time is being well spent. This direct application of the MKIS can also demonstrate its utility to the system.

A second reason special consideration should be given to training senior managers is that some top-level executives may fear loss of respect if they are trained by a subordinate or if others see them making mistakes. To avoid these risks, it may be necessary to plan private sessions in the executive's office and to assign training of senior executives to the top management representative on the MKIS team. One useful approach may be to develop training exercises that correspond to the documentation so that top-level executives can train themselves.

FEEDBACK

Feedback is the process by which users provide information to developers on the performance of the MKIS system and ways to improve it. It is a fundamental part of the implementation process because it identifies the need for change and allows the system to remain adaptable. Although the system has been tested, ways of improving the system—and perhaps even new bugs—are likely to be discovered as more people use the system and gain experience with its functions. If this feedback is shared with the system developers, then changes can be made to enhance the operation of the system and make it more satisfying to users.

To take advantage of these user experiences, the MKIS developers need to establish an easy way for users to make suggestions. An electronic-mail suggestion box, for instance, may be a simple yet effective way to obtain user feedback on the current MKIS system. Suggestions can be reviewed by the system administrator, and if a pattern is noted or a problem is discovered, the administrator can begin an investigation and review with the MKIS team the suggestions and possible actions. The administrator can also maintain an electronic bulletin board to inform users of changes in the system and of other users' ideas. Users who read these ideas may be encouraged to communicate their own experiences. Users' comments on the administrator's ideas for addressing problems or improving the system should also be invited and can help to refine plans.

Feedback is also important because an effective MKIS must be able to adapt as the marketing environment changes and as marketing decision processes improve. The organization, the marketing department, and the MKIS must all adapt to changing internal and external environments. Periodic marketing audits, occasional meetings with marketing managers and staffs, and reviews of users' comments in a MKIS suggestion box will all provide ideas that can suggest opportunities. These can be explored further and may lead to improvements in the MKIS system.

MODIFICATIONS

Modifications are defined as all changes to the system after it is installed. The procedures for handling modifications to the system vary, depending upon the seriousness of the changes that must be made. There are three types of modifications:

- Modifications that involve small adjustments to correct bugs
- Modifications that involve substantial efforts to correct significant system errors
- Modifications that involve developing new modules to provide new capabilities

Modifications to Correct Bugs

The first type of modification is when a minor reprogramming effort is required to correct an error in the system that does not change the user interface. This type of modification may be treated as a part of the routine system maintenance process. Although the possible impacts of the bug should be investigated and reported to users to ensure that the bug has not caused inappropriate decisions or provided erroneous information, correcting the problem is the responsibility of the system administrator and the MKIS technical support staff.

Modifications to Correct System Errors

The second type of modification also involves correcting errors in the system, but the effort required to correct the error is more substantial. As with the first type of modification, the MKIS team must study the possible impact of the problem on marketing decisions and announce warnings if necessary. In this type of situation, however, it will also be necessary to estimate the resources and time required to develop and implement the changes. The seriousness of the problem and the amount of organizational resources that may be needed require the system administrator to review the situation with top management and obtain support. As the changes are made on a test system, the new user interfaces and procedures should be evaluated by users of the original module in the marketing department. After the modifications have passed all reviews, the new system can be phased in with new documentation and user training.

Developing New Modules

The third type of modification involves developing new modules that will provide the MKIS with new capabilities. The idea for a new module may begin with users' suggestions, requests from marketing managers, or recommendations from information system professionals. Whatever the source, if the initial review of the idea justifies support from the system administrator and the MKIS team, then the recommendations should be developed into macrospecifications, just as in the planning stage of the MKIS creation process reviewed earlier in this book. This step is necessary because the macrospecifications that will document the new module must be developed to ensure that it will achieve its goals and guide the technical development stage.

The objectives of the new module must be defined and presented with the macrospecifications to top management for approval and for the commitment of financial and human resources. This type of continuing renewal of support from top management is needed to verify that the information system's resources are properly allocated relative to the goals and priorities of the organization and to ensure that accountability is maintained in all MKIS activities.

In all three types of modifications—whether corrections of minor bugs, corrections or enhancements of current modules that affect user interfaces, or the development of major new modules to support changing marketing needs—careful attention must be given to the impacts of the modifications on users and on other parts of the system. Extensive testing should be carried out with programs and procedures used prior to the changes and with the new programs so that results may be compared. Careful analysis is needed to verify that an adjustment to one aspect of the system does not result in a new error elsewhere.

SUMMARY

In this chapter we have considered the four basic activities involved in the implementation of a marketing information system. These activities are phased implementation, user training, feedback, and modifications. As each new MKIS module is introduced, these activities will be repeated to help users adapt to the new resources and to ensure that new modules operate correctly.

In the first step, phased implementation, the users of the MKIS and the organization as a whole can benefit from progress as it is made rather than waiting for a holistic system to be installed. Then, because the users of the MKIS are concerned with the practical benefits of the system in regard to their own work roles, task-oriented documentation should be developed for the MKIS modules. This type of documentation is organized around the basic operations users must carry out to perform specifically marketing-related tasks.

Through the processes of feedback and modification, the system is debugged and desirable enhancements are identified, approved, and developed. The system administrator should devise procedures for monitoring users' comments and recommendations regarding the MKIS and for reviewing this feedback with the MKIS team to determine which should be acted on and with what level of urgency.

The MKIS implementation process does not have an ending point. Modifications will be ongoing as conditions change and as users generate more effective ways of carrying out analyses. As an ongoing system, the MKIS must be designed to adapt to the needs of users so that it will remain an asset to the organization in the search for competitive advantage.

Key Terms

feedback	*phased conversion*	*task-oriented documentation*
modifications		

READINGS FOR MORE INFORMATION ON TOPICS IN CHAPTER 9

Cash, J. I., R. G. Eccles, N. Nohria, and R. L. Nolan (1993). *Building the Information Age Organization: Structure, Control, and Information Technologies*. Homewood, IL: Irwin.

Fortune (1993b). "Making It All Worker-Friendly." *Fortune*, Special Issue, Vol. 128, No. 7 (Autumn), pp. 44–53.

Ives, B., and M. Olson (1984). "User Involvement and MIS Success: A Review of Research." *Management Science*, Vol. 30, No. 5 (May), pp. 586–603.

Where Do We Go from Here?

10

In this short book on marketing information systems, we have considered how modern organizations can capitalize on the recent explosion of marketing information to create competitive advantage. We have considered the data available to marketing managers as a result of routine business activities and the wealth of external data resources that can guide marketing tactics and strategy. We have also seen that this vast wealth of data creates its own problems, which require carefully developed database management and decision support systems that can help managers focus on and interpret the relevant data. Such systems range from reporting and inquiry systems to analytical models, expert systems, and even neural networks. Finally, we have considered the planning, technical development, and implementation stages of creating a MKIS and the procedures needed to ensure a successful project.

CONTINUING TRENDS IN COMPUTING

Where do we go from here? The information explosion is revolutionizing marketing practice (Perreault, 1992; Blattberg, Glazer, and Little, 1994), and it is not over yet. Three trends seem to characterize the recent history of computing, all of which we can expect to continue. These trends are

- continued improvement in data collection and dissemination;
- increased computing power in terms of speed of processing, data storage, and data access; and,
- the development of "intelligent," user-friendly decision support software to guide data interpretation and usage.

These trends are not just changing how marketing is practiced; they are also changing the skill set that will be required for marketers to do their jobs. Now, while marketers must continue to develop expertise in the traditional marketing research paradigm involving the fundamentals of primary data collection and analysis (Green, 1992), they must at the same time keep abreast of the new information resources and data management and interpretation tools that will be developed during the next decade. Let us consider more specifically how each of the above trends may influence the marketer's work in the future.

Data Collection and Dissemination

If any one technological advance can be singled out as the major contributor to the emerging new paradigm of marketing research and management (Malhotra, 1992; Perreault, 1992), it is the development of scanner systems and bar codes. Today, automatic identification data collection systems based on scanner and bar code technologies are the primary data collection method for processing and recording sales and inventories and for tracing the movement of goods through distribution channels. Automatic identification data collection systems are not limited to recording product sales and store location. In combination with credit card purchases, sales can actually be tracked back to individual customers. With this data, a diligent analyst can construct targeted consumer profiles and develop individual, personalized offerings. This type of information analysis is already being done with the support of expert systems, and we can expect such applications to grow in frequency and sophistication in the future.

Continued improvement in data collection will be coupled with continued improvement in the dissemination of data on potential customers' buying habits. Today, the technology needed to support the ongoing collection of consumer and organizational buyer behavior data is still capital- and labor-intensive. Private firms engaged in data collection activities have a strong interest in expanding the utility of their data resources to greater numbers of marketing clients. This, in turn, will spur the development of systems to make data more easily accessible, at a fee, to all organizations. These systems will provide enhanced data communications capabilities, including speed, accuracy, and highly user-friendly interfaces for on-line data inquiries, identification of subsets of data of interest, and transferral of data to clients' computer systems. Moreover, the popularization of data will challenge the savvy marketer more than ever to make the best possible use of data to create and maintain competitive advantage.

The technology of digital computing is advancing faster than guidelines for its application. This lag is particularly true of ethical guidelines (Mason, 1986). Privacy is a key ethical issue that the profession of marketing and individual marketing practitioners must confront (Bloom, Adler, and Milne, 1994; Bessen, 1993; Davis, 1992; Rothfeder, 1992; Simon, 1992). Unless this issue is appropriately addressed, the marketing profession risks having legal and regulatory guidelines imposed, and these might thwart potentially profitable and appropriate uses of the new data resources.

Increased Computer Power

Each year since the advent of desktop computers in the late 1970s, we have witnessed exponential growth in the power of computer hardware. At the supercomputer, mainframe, midrange, and microcomputer levels, the power and speed of microprocessors have increased, while the costs of data storage have declined dramatically. This evolution is likely to continue. Even as we think the advances may level off, the industry announces new rounds of technological innovations to increase computing power while decreasing costs. In short, computer hardware is keeping up with the growing data loads that enhancements in data collection are generating.

Increases in computing power at declining costs have two important implications. First, the improving cost-benefit ratios of computing hardware will add further impetus to the popularization of marketing data access and use. As more and more organizations—large and small—find that the hardware resources needed to build effective MKIS are affordable, they will seek to gain the competitive advantages that effective data utilization promises. Subsequently, more marketers will seek to effectively utilize the new and expanding information resources. Natural increases in competitive pressures will force even the most reluctant members of the profession to incorporate MKIS into their organizations' plans.

Second, as marketing information systems are seen as increasingly practical investments, a growing market will develop for decision support software to improve the efficiency of MKIS data management and utilization. This leads to the third trend, the development of intelligent, user-friendly decision support software.

Intelligent, User-Friendly Software

As noted, access to data and hardware has created the opportunity for a growing market for decision support software. Even today, marketing and information systems professionals in academic life are directing more attention to techniques for analyzing the volumes of scanner and single-source data that are available. This will continue and will be supplemented by the development of data analysis techniques and products in private industry. As new techniques develop, we can expect that they either will become commercial products themselves or will stimulate the development of commercial products, just as the CoverStory system from Ocean Spray Cranberries and Information Resources, Inc., evolved into a commercial product.

The volume of data that is available will also lead to new analytical approaches to take advantage of its potential for improving marketing decision making. We have already seen great innovations in the development of environmental scanning systems that can, at least partially, automate information search and scanning processes (e.g., CoverStory). This, in turn, saves managers time and allows them to focus their attention on critical trends. Whereas in the past, available analytical techniques drove the data collection process, in the future, the data collection capabilities of marketing organizations and their supporting agencies will drive the development of data analysis and decision support tools.

HOW MARKETING WILL CHANGE

How will marketing change as a result of these continuing trends? One can only speculate. We do know that these trends will continue and can be expected to change the marketing focus of modern organizations. The new data resources provide several possible scenarios, three of which we will consider here:

- Micromarketing and customized marketing
- Interbrand competition in mass marketing
- Tactically differentiated products for segmented and rapidly changing markets

Micromarketing and Customized Marketing

First, we believe that greater knowledge about individual customers will lead some organizations to focus on **micromarketing** and **customized marketing** as the marketing offer is designed for the specific customer (Ingram, 1992; Winters, 1990). This trend toward individuals is at least implied by Blattberg and Glazer in their essay "Marketing in the Information Revolution" (1994). Recall too that micromarketing is behind the recent success of firms such as Dell Computers.

Blattberg and Glazer (1994) see the information revolution opening a new stage in business evolution. In this stage, the marketing organizations that are successful in controlling the customer will be those that serve as **systems integrators**. Systems integrators use information systems to simplify the customer's buying process by combining products from several sources to create a product-package of value to customers. This trend will further shift the emphasis of some modern businesses from mass production products to customization and customer support and satisfaction.

The micromarketing scenario is appropriate for relatively high-cost products that can be produced as sets of modular components with low customization costs (Blattberg and Glazer, 1994). In this approach, information about the customer and his or her identity is crucial, as is direct communication between the customer and the organization. Information about the customer allows customization of products through modularization of component parts. While this is possible today, future information systems will greatly enhance communication between customers and the manufacturer of the end product and will provide manufacturers with greater abilities to market products directly to customers.

The new information systems resources discussed in this book have implications for distribution channel members as well. Today, retailers and, to a lesser extent, wholesalers and industrial distributors control the customer in the sense of being the points of contact between the manufacturer and the customer. The new information systems may provide a strategic window of opportunity for current retailers and wholesalers to take advantage of their position in the flow of information to position themselves as systems integrators that provide customized products.

Interbrand Competition

In the second scenario, the future holds increased **interbrand competition** in mass marketing, where the focal point shifts from the customer to the competition. This trend might be appropriate for low-cost, undifferentiated, repeat-purchase products in deeply penetrated markets. The new marketing information resources may help these types of competitors to continually monitor each other's tactics and constantly reassess their own situations and marketing tactics, including pricing moves, sales promotions, advertising campaigns, and new product introductions. Decision support systems will aid in the interpretation of store, sales, and customer data to suggest tactical responses to competitors' moves and to recommend adjustments to one's own strategy as the battles for shares of saturated markets are waged.

Tactically Differentiated Products

In a third scenario, the ideas of customization of the marketing offer to specific customers and competitive mass marketing blend together to suggest **tactically differentiated products** for segmented and rapidly changing markets. This is the type of situation depicted by Perreault (1992) in his description of the operations of the retail clothing chain The Limited. This organization continuously monitors sales to guide marketing decisions that drive electronically distributed orders to manufacturing operations scattered across the globe. The key to success for The Limited is integrating manufacturing with store sales data to provide not only just-in-time inventory but just-in-time manufacturing as well. By providing continous marketing data to systems with the decision support capabilities to translate the data into decision-relevant information for managerial decision making, this modern MKIS allows The Limited to rapidly respond to fads and fashions and thereby gain competitive advantage by being the "first" to meet the newest demand. As less expensive decision support tools become available, we may expect to see many more examples of such tactically responsive marketing information systems.

SUMMARY

Although there are other ways in which MKIS-related technological changes might influence marketing practice, it should be clear from our brief overview that today's information systems technologies offer great promise for adaptable, innovative organizations to gain competitive advantage. The resources and tools marketing managers will use in the future will also increase the need for managers to be innovators themselves as they meet tomorrow's technological challenges. Marketing information systems will become a staple of business practice, and business activities will be faster and more competitive. If nothing else, we can be certain that the future will not be "business as usual" and that well planned and developed MKIS resources will be a key to survival and growth.

Key Terms

customized marketing

interbrand competition

micromarketing

systems integrators

tactically differentiated products

READINGS FOR MORE INFORMATION ON TOPICS IN CHAPTER 10

Bessen, J. (1993). "Riding the Marketing Information Wave." *Harvard Business Review*, Vol. 71, No. 5 (September–October), pp. 150–160.

Blattberg, R. C., and R. Glazer (1994). "Marketing in the Information Revolution." In R. C. Blattberg, R. Glazer, and J. D. C. Little, *The Marketing Information Revolution*. Boston: Harvard Business School Press.

Malhotra, N. K. (1992). "Shifting Perspective on the Shifting Paradigm in Marketing Research: A New Paradigm in Marketing Research." *Journal of the Academy of Marketing Science*, Vol. 20, No. 4 (Fall), pp. 379–387.

Perreault, W. D., Jr. (1992). "The Shifting Paradigm in Marketing Research." *Journal of the Academy of Marketing Science*, Vol. 20, No. 4 (Fall), pp. 367–375.

Appendix[‡]
Database Concepts

[‡] This appendix represents the joint work of Kimball P. Marshall and Roger A. Pick.

Throughout this book, our goal has been to provide you with a readable, comprehensive review of the data resources, components, and development processes of marketing information systems. Because this book has been written for audiences that include business students and practitioners who might not be familiar with the language of information systems, we have generally avoided discussions that are too technical or full of information systems jargon. We hope, however, that this book will stimulate a desire for further study of marketing information systems. As you read other sources of information, such as those we have suggested at the end of each chapter and in the bibliography, you may encounter some technical ideas and language that have not been addressed in this book. To help you, we have provided this appendix as a database primer—an introduction to the basic concepts and language of databases.

Three main topics are presented in this Appendix:

- The elements of data sets and data files
- Types of database files
- Relational databases

THE ELEMENTS OF DATA SETS AND DATA FILES

Information is knowledge that can be used to guide purposive decision making. In a computer-based information system, information is recorded as data items in a data set. The term **data** is defined here as the symbolic and interpretable representation of information. A **data item** is one element of information stored in a data set. A **data set** is a well-organized collection of information that is symbolically represented as data items. For example, if a data set contains demographic information on a customer, the age of the customer might be one data item. Data sets stored in computer memory are called **data files**. A **database** is a well-organized collection of data files that can be used in conjunction with one another. Because we will be referring to data to be stored in computer systems, we will use the terms *data set* and *data file* interchangeably.

How Data is Represented in Computers

Computer systems store data in **binary code**, arrays of 0s and 1s for which the specific arrangment of the 0s and 1s is interpretable by the computer as part of or all of a data item or instruction. **Bits** are single-element binary codes that stand for 0 or 1 or an on-off switch. **Bytes** in modern conventional computer systems are sets of eight bits interpreted together in a fixed sequence. Each bit in a byte may take on a value of 0 or 1. When the values of the bits are considered in sequence, up to 256 unique patterns of eight 0s and 1s can be created. This is called *hexadecimal representation*. These 256 patterns allow a byte to represent any one of up to 256 unique symbols to a computer. In a simple character image data set, each character would require one byte. The term **character image** is used because each symbol is a computer-interpretable character. The image of this character can usually be displayed on the computer screen.

For the sake of simplicity, we will assume in this discussion that all information in a data set is encoded as character image data represented by one or more adjacent bytes, with the bytes representing alphanumeric, numeric, and special symbols. Be aware, however, that data is often stored in more sophisticated formats, such as binary-coded system files developed for specific applications programs. These approaches to data storage are often more efficient from a computer processing standpoint, but from a user standpoint, the one-byte-per-character style described here is a valid and practical approach to visualizing how data is organized.

A set of adjacent symbols that should be interpreted together is called a **field**. For example, if a person's age is 21 years and the numeric symbols "2" and "1" are stored adjacent to one another as "21", then they represent a field. Data items are contained in fields specified by the person constructing and maintaining the data set. The term **database administrator** refers to the person with the responsibility for constructing the data sets in a database and for maintaining the integrity, accuracy, and accessibility of the data.

The symbols used to represent information may be numeric, alphabetical, or some other special character. **Numeric data** is visually represented by numeral symbols that have the properties of a number system—meaning that the information can be ordered from greater to lesser magnitude. Once read by the computer and interpreted as numbers, the data is represented as binary numbers and stored in binary-coded system files. For simplicity's sake, it is adequate for our purposes to continue to think of numbers in their numeral symbol form.

Alphabetical data is data that uses symbols—called *characters*—from an alphabet. A **special character** is a nonnumeric and nonalphabetical symbol that can be recognized by a computer system, such as the symbol "#". Alphabetical symbols, special characters, and number symbols can all be used as codes and are referred to as **alphanumeric data**. **Codes** are symbolic abbreviations that represent information.

The term **value** is used to refer to the symbols contained in a data item. For example, information about a person might include the person's gender, and the letter "M" might serve as the code for "male". Alphabetical data that has human-language properties is referred to as **text data**. Text data can be a word, a sentence, a paragraph, or an entire document.

The well-organized nature of a data set is an important characteristic because it distinguishes data sets from random collections of symbols whose information content, if any, cannot be interpreted. The data items in a data set must be systematically organized, and the method of organization and the symbolic meaning of the codes must be documented so that the meaning of the data items can be interpreted by humans and by the computer programs that will be used to process the data.

A **data dictionary** is the formal, written documentation that identifies and defines all data items and describes the organization of the data file. The data dictionary may exist in a printed paper form and as a file on the computer system that can be used by programs to access the data. For simple data sets, the data dictionary is sometimes referred to as a **codebook**. A **database manager** is a computer program that uses the data dictionary corresponding to the data files in a database to coordinate access to the data in the database.

From Data Items to Records in Files

In a simple data set, the data items are organized into records. A **record** is a set of data items that refer to the same entity. An **entity** is the unit of analysis to which the information in the data items of a record refer. For example, if a data set is constructed to represent all of a store's customers who have charge accounts and the data items to be included for each customer are the customer name, address, phone number, and account number, the entity to which each record refers is the customer. In a well-organized data set, each customer is placed in a different record. The customer's name, address, phone number, and account number would be the data items contained in the record. To avoid confusion, each record should contain information on only one entity.

In Chapter 5 we used the term *level of aggregation* to refer to the degree to which data items in a record represent specific entities or events rather than a summary of many entities or events. To illustrate this concept further, suppose a data set contains records on a company's individual salespeople, with each record containing information on only one salesperson. Suppose also that within each record, one field contains the salesperson's total sales for the month and another field contains the identification number of the sales office to which the salesperson is assigned. A new data set can be created by summarizing the sales of all of the salespersons in each office. This new data set would contain the sales office identification number and the total sales for that office. Therefore, while the level of aggregation in the first data set is the salesperson, in the new data set the level of aggregation would be the sales office.

To avoid confusion, a record should generally contain information on only one entity and only one level of aggregation. There are occasions, however, when a record might contain aggregated data and data on a single entity. For instance, continuing with the sales data example from above, an analyst might want to add the sales office total onto a salesperson's record as a new data item so that he or she can compare it with the salesperson's individual total.

A simple data set can be illustrated as a data matrix. A **data matrix** is an arrangement of data into rows and columns, in which the rows represent the entities for which data are recorded and the columns represent specific data items. These columns are also known as **variables**. A variable is a specific type of data item that is represented on each record of a data set. The values of a variable can vary from record to record. In our example above, the salesperson's total could be considered a variable. The cells in the data matrix represent the fields containing the data items.

Figure A.1 illustrates a simple data set as a data matrix. This data set has five variables: salesperson identification number, sales office identification number, total sales, and year, month, and day. The entity, or unit of analysis, is the salesperson. The level of aggregation is the individual salesperson.

			Variables			
	Salesperson ID Number	Sales Office ID	Total Sales	Year	Month	Day
Field positions	1–3	4–5	6–10	11–12	13–14	15–16
Records	001	01	18959	94	10	15
	002	01	21654	94	10	15
	003	02	55432	94	10	15
	004	02	43789	94	10	15
	005	03	32421	94	10	15
	006	03	29743	94	10	15

FIGURE A.1   A Simple Data Matrix

Record Formats

If a computer system is to read the data items on a record, it must have a way to identify which symbols represent which data items. The **record format** refers to how the data in a record and data file is organized so that the specific data items can be distinguished. Two basic types of record formats are fixed-field character image and delimited-field character image formats. In a **fixed-field character image format**, all of the records of the data file have the same arrangement of data items, and the number of symbols used to represent a data item is the same for all records. The number of symbols allocated to a data item is called the **field width**. In our example, the salesperson's total sales might be allocated up to nine characters. If the value of a data item for a specific record does not take that much space, leading or trailing blanks are used to fill the unused spaces.

Because a fixed-field character image format defines the fixed width of each data item and the data items are arranged in the same order on all records, the position of each field on any record can be described to a computer program by specifying the locations of the beginning and ending positions in an array of sequential positions equal to the record length. Each position is equal to one byte of space in a computer record. These records are called **fixed-length records** because the total record length is the same for all records in the data file and equals the sum of the sizes of the fields.

In a **delimited-field character image format**, the data items are arrayed in the same sequence for all records, but the sizes of the individual fields can change from record to record in the data file depending on the number of symbols needed. As a result, the lengths of the records vary as well. Accordingly, records in a data file of this type are called **variable-length records**. In the delimited-field character image format, the position of each data item is defined to a computer program by specifying (1) the sequential location of the data item (e.g., the third, fourth, or fifth item in the sequence), (2) the format, and (3) a special character to serve as an indicator that one data item's field has ended and the next is about to begin. The special character is called the **delimiter**. It must be a symbol that will not be used in any part of a code for any data item in the data file.

With either type of record format, as well as with the more sophisticated systems for recording data alluded to earlier, the basic imagery of a data matrix can help the unsophisticated user visualize the data and how it is arranged in a data file.

Now that we understand how data items are organized into records and data files, we can turn our attention to the various types of files commonly used in modern business databases.

TYPES OF DATABASE FILES

To understand database systems, we must consider database files from both a managerial and a technical perspective. The *managerial* viewpoint considers the different ways in which files are used. The *technical* viewpoint considers how files are stored and their data accessed. From either viewpoint, a **file** is an aggregation of data managed as a unit by the computer's operating system.

Managerial File Types

From a data management or administrative perspective, we can identify six general types of files that might be used to maintain a MKIS database:

- Master files
- Transaction files
- Entry files
- Log files
- Backup files
- Archival files

Although this list of file types is not intended to be comprehensive (other types of files might be defined during the MKIS development process), it provides a good overview of the various types of files common to MKIS and business transactions databases.

A **master file** contains semipermanent information about an entity. For example, a customer file might contain customer names, addresses, telephone numbers, credit terms, outstanding debt, and the date of each customer's most recent purchase.

A **transaction file** contains a series of changes that will be applied to a master file or another data set in the database in order to update the database. For example, a transaction file might contain a list of purchases. This list would be used to update the customer file by changing the appropriate records for the amount owed and the last date a purchase was made.

An **entry file** is a transaction file that has not yet been validated. For example, the list of purchases mentioned above would be an entry file until the list has been checked to remove any absurd values most likely caused by an entry error. The check includes verifying that each customer number matches that of an actual customer, each product number matches that of an actual product, quantities are all entered as nonnegative integers, dates correspond to valid dates, and all numeric quantities are in ranges that are reasonable for the meaning of the field.

A **log file** is a list of changes made to the master file. Conceptually, the log file is a compilation of all past transaction files. Log files can be used for auditing purposes and to reconstruct a master file whose contents were destroyed.

A **backup file** is a complete copy of a single file at a single point in time. If a customer file is accidentally lost, it can be reconstructed in an up-to-date state with a backup copy from some point in the past plus a log file containing all the changes made since the last backup. Because many of the accidents that destroy a master file (e.g., a fire or a flood) will destroy *all* of the files at the master file's location, it is important that backup files be stored in a secure, off-site location.

Archival files are files that have no current importance but are retained for legal or tax reasons or for future analysis. It is important to maintain a record retention policy that defines when files become archives and when those archives should be deleted.

Technical File Types

On a basic technical level, files can be classified as either sequential or direct. A **sequential file** is one in which the records must be read by the computer in the same order in which they were written. A **direct file**, on the other hand, allows the computer to directly access and read any record in the file, independent of the order in which the records were written. The benefits of sequential files are that they can be implemented using inexpensive hardware, are easy to understand, and are easily programmed. Direct files usually include some sort of lookup scheme—usually an associated index—that allows the user to determine which record contains a desired data item. An index speeds retrieval of data but slows updating data because each change must be made to both the file and its index. An index also requires more storage space.

RELATIONAL DATABASES

A **data model** is a way of structuring data and the relationships among files so that data from various files can be used together. A common data model that is particularly useful for addressing MKIS data management issues is the relational database model. As noted in Chapter 1, a **relational database** is an organized set of data in which the various types of data items are sufficiently identified by a predetermined set of criteria so that items may be linked together in a logical way.

In a relational database, data is stored in a collection of rectangular tables whose contents change over time. Each table can be a data file, or several tables can be held in a single data file. Each of these tables is a data matrix with the columns representing variables and the rows representing specific entities for which data has been collected. In the language of databases, a table is called a *relation* and each row is called a *tuple* (Davis and Olson, 1985, pp. 123–125; McFadden and Hoffer, 1991, pp. 20, 112–113).

Flexibility in both content and use are important benefits of a relational database. For example, the database can be expanded to include new variables by adding columns to a table or by adding new tables. While the number of tables and the number of columns in each table are fairly fixed in that they do not change moment by moment, when changing business conditions require that more variables be added, the numbers of tables or columns can be changed to accommodate the new requirements. Of course, these changes must be documented.

Certain columns in a relational database are called key columns. A **key column**, or **key variable**, is a column or set of columns for which the contents of those columns alone uniquely identify a particular row, or entity, in a relational database and the values of the remaining columns, or variables, for that row can be read. By using key columns to link together data from separate data matrices, the researcher gains great flexibility in selecting combinations of information on entities for analysis. One useful application of the properties of relational databases and their key variables is *modular component analysis* (Dunne and Wolk, 1977), discussed in Chapter 5.

To illustrate this concept, suppose that data is stored in a collection of rectangular data matrices. Certain key variables contained as data items in the various data sets identify specific entities or entity types and their aggregation levels. The key variables can change from one application to another, but the appropriate key variables for any given application must be contained in all of the data files that are to be related to one another. By using the key variables, data from different files can be combined and data may be aggregated to a higher level. In the salesperson's example we used earlier, the sales office identification number served as a key variable.

In that example, the sales total for each salesperson was used to compute the total sales by sales office. The sales office identification number, as a key variable, was used to identify which salespeople belonged to which sales office. The result was a data matrix with two data items, or variables, and with one record for each sales office. The variables are the sales office identification number and the total sales for that office. In this new data set, the sales office is both the entity and the level of aggregation. Since the key variable—the sales office identification number—exists on both the sales office data set and the salesperson data set, it can be used to relate the two data sets together so that the sales office total could be added onto the salesperson data set as a new data item. This was done in the earlier example.

Although combining two levels of aggregation in a data set can create confusion, it might be required for many types of analyses. For example, by including the sales office total in the salesperson data set, an analyst can compare each salesperson's performance with total office sales and can compute the percentage that each salesperson contributed to her or his office total.

FINAL CONSIDERATIONS

In this Appendix we have provided a brief introduction to the fundamental concepts of databases as they might be applied to marketing information systems. Do not be misled by the simplicity of this introduction. Database design and management are complex processes, and the effective development of the required databases is crucial to the short- and long-term successes of a MKIS. The database administrator must be a highly trained, experienced information systems professional who is able to spend considerable time monitoring and maintaining the utility and integrity of the MKIS databases. Although formal responsibility for database management rests with the MKIS database administrator, the more marketing managers know about the topics introduced in this Appendix, the more they can contribute to MKIS planning, development, and implementation. This is particularly true in regard to relational databases.

As we have noted in several locations throughout this book, relational databases and data sets designed with the lowest possible level of aggregation provide the greatest flexibility for addressing the unstructured and ad hoc questions that are intrinsic to marketing management. While such database designs may require more computer processing time than other approaches, the benefits can be extensive.

Modern database management systems typically provide the aggregation and data merging capabilities we have described. You may want to explore microcomputer-based products such as dBase and Paradox as a way of developing a working familiarity with the concepts discussed here. Even statistical program packages such as SAS and SPSS can provide the ability to aggregate data and merge files using key variables in data files and thus may serve as relational database managers. You are also encouraged to explore these systems as a way of broadening your understanding of this extremely important topic.

Glossary of Key Concepts

A

Accounts receivable systems Keep track of which customers owe how much money for what goods and services. The major subfunctions are invoicing, billing, receiving payment, and correcting entries.

Administrative supports Provide the guidelines, processes, procedures, and personnel needed to maintain system integrity and to support managers using the system.

Alternative history model A special form of **simulation model**, in which a historical event is examined and predictions are made regarding what might have occurred under different historical conditions.

Analytical model A computer program that considers *why* marketing events have occurred, predicts future events, and selects the best among several alternative marketing decisions.

Applications software The programs marketing managers use to access data in the database system and to analyze the data so as to provide information to guide marketing decisions.

Artificial intelligence The use of a computer to accomplish tasks that require a human being's intelligence when she or he performs those same tasks.

Artificial intelligence systems Computer systems that carry out goal-oriented decision-making processes by drawing on and interpreting information derived from past experiences of human beings, data on past events, and, possibly, the experiences of the system itself.

B

Balance forward system An accounting system in which the firm keeps track only of the total amount the customer owes; payments reduce that total.

Boundary department An interface department that links an organization to its environment in order to create opportunities for exchange.

Business partners Companies involved in the value chain with whom the organization has or expects to have a formal relationship. This relationship may involve supplying products, transporting and warehousing goods, selling goods, and providing customer services.

C

Central processing unit (CPU) The microprocessors that carry out the computational and logical work of a computer system, along with related electronic memory devices and interfaces to other equipment.

Competitive environment The structural features of the industry and the activities and capabilities of competitors. Specific issues include such concerns as production costs, economies of scale, extent of product differentiation, capital requirements, distribution channels, and power of suppliers. Specific competitors' market shares, brand recognition, customer loyalty, and technological advantages should also be studied.

Concurrent verbalization A **knowledge acquisition** technique in which the expert in the application domain is asked to verbalize his or her thoughts continuously throughout the problem-solving process for the **knowledge engineer**, who then uses this process to build an **expert system**.

Conditional forecast model A type of **forecast model** in which past data is used to predict future events, but in this type of model the assumptions about the circumstances under which the predictions are expected to hold true are explicitly built into the model.

Consumer scanner panel data The data sets resulting from a group of consumers participating in long-term research about their purchases. The purchase data is collected using point-of-sale automatic identification scanner systems.

Customer environment Includes the organization's current and potential customers.

Customer service systems Systems designed with the primary goal of tracking problems customers have with an organization's products and arranging procedures to correct the problem so as to satisfy the customer.

D

Data dictionary A formal document that identifies and defines all data items, describes the organization of the data files that will be used by the MKIS, and integrates these into a common database system.

Database A well-organized collection of data files that can be used in conjunction with one another.

Decision support system (DSS) The set of "problem-solving technology consisting of people, knowledge, software, and hardware successfully wired into the management process" (Little, 1990) to facilitate improved decision making by marketing managers.

Defensive intelligence An aspect of an organization's strategic intelligence system that monitors environments to avoid surprises and to verify the organization's assumptions.

Drill-down capability A function of an **executive support system** that allows the executive to look at the details behind a number, breaking them down into their lower **levels of aggregation** as needed.

E

Economic environments The financial and monetary systems that influence the firm and its markets.

Electronic data interchanges (EDI) The transmission of standard business documents and information by electronic means.

Environmental analysis The process of assessing and interpreting data gathered in **environmental scanning** regarding an organization's environment.

Environmental scanning The process of monitoring the environment for events that may influence the organization.

Exception report A type of **reporting and inquiry system** in which one or more quantitative indicators of business performance are reported and compared to a "standard."

Executive support system (ESS) A special type of **decision support system** that combines **reporting and inquiry** systems with **analytical modeling** capabilities in a highly user-friendly format. Its purpose is to allow managers to easily review business performance indicators and explore their implications for future decisions.

Expert systems A type of **artificial intelligence system** that uses the knowledge of experts as input information. Essentially, these software applications mimic the logic of the decision processes of human experts.

Expert system programming shell A computer program that assists in the writing and execution of an expert system.

External data Information provided by sources outside the company.

F

Feedback The process by which users provide information to developers on the performance of the MKIS system and ways to improve it.

Focus group A collection of several persons—typically eight to ten—who are asked to address a specific topic in a group interview.

Forecast model A type of **analytical model** that uses mathematical algorithms and logical propositions to interpret data in order to predict future events.

4Ps of marketing Product, price, promotion, and place, where *place* refers to the distribution system activities. Also known as the **marketing mix**.

G

Geographic data mapping system An approach to **inquiry systems** that allows data coded with an address, zip code, or longitude and latitude coordinates to be located and displayed on a geographic map.

Group decision support system (GDSS) A computer-based **decision support system** that assists with problem-solving activities involving multiple decision makers. A GDSS integrates reporting and inquiry systems with analytical models to support decision making and provides software to support electronic meetings and facilitate group interaction, determine group preferences, generate information from the individuals in the group, and process the information the group generates.

I

Inbound logistics How the firm obtains needed resources from the environment and from suppliers.

Inquiry system Computer-based **decision support system** that allows a manager to obtain desired information from an appropriate database when that information is needed.

Integrity The ability of the MKIS system to function as expected and to provide accurate data and analytical techniques.

Intelligence Purposive decision-making processes that are based on consideration of relevant and available data and past experiences, carried out with the intention of achieving specified goals.

Internal data Information collected by the firm on a regular basis as a routine part of business activities, including internal movement of resources among departments and exchanges with the outside environment.

Internal environment Includes the managers who use the MKIS system, the types of decisions they must make, the corporate objectives that must guide decisions and the overall decision-making process, and the cultural, social, and internal political factors that influence the organization's activities and decision making.

K

Knowledge acquisition The process of gaining knowledge from the domain expert for use in the expert system.

Knowledge engineer A computer programmer-analyst who specializes in expert system development.

L

Lead Name and way of contacting a potential customer who may have an interest in a product.

Lead tracking systems Procedures for generating leads, qualifying a lead as a **prospect**, and tracking the outcome of contacts.

Level of aggregation The degree to which data represents specific entities or events rather than a summary of many entities or events.

M

Macrospecifications The broad definitions of the system requirements of the intended users.

Market An organization's set of potential customers.

Market segments Groups of potential customers with similar needs or buying characteristics.

Marketing The process of executing the conception, pricing, promotion, and distribution of ideas, goods, and services to create exchanges that satisfy individual and organizational goals.

Marketing audit A comprehensive review of marketing activities, information needs, and decision-making processes.

Marketing functions audit Detailed audits of specific functional areas—such as advertising, pricing, sales, or product management—that the **marketing systems audit** or **marketing productivity audit** indicates have serious problems.

Marketing information system (MKIS): A comprehensive and flexible, formal and ongoing system designed to provide an organized flow of relevant information to guide marketing decision making.

Marketing mix The controllable variables an organization puts together that will appeal to customers. Also known as the **4 Ps of marketing**.

Marketing organization audit Focuses on the current effectiveness of the marketing department and related departments (e.g., sales), as well as on the effectiveness of working relationships between marketing and other divisions.

Marketing productivity audit Focuses on the costs of marketing activities and seeks justification for expenditures.

Marketing research Provides data to support marketing decision making. It is distinguished from MKIS in that it is intended to provide in-depth information collected over a fixed, relatively short period of time.

Marketing strategies audit Reviews decisions and plans regarding in which markets to participate and with which products, philosophies regarding how to differentiate the company and its products from competitors and their products, and objectives that focus on exploiting strengths and overcoming weaknesses.

Marketing systems audit Allows for the assessment of procedures for such activities as sales forecasting, establishing sales goals and quotas, physical distribution, product development, product elimination, and assessing advertising effectiveness.

Model A mathematical or logical representation of a real system or part of a real system.

Modifications Changes to the MKIS system after it is installed.

Modular component analysis A process of assessing the profit or revenue contribution made by product sales at each **level of aggregation**.

N

Neural networks Computer applications that mimic the human brain. One important aspect of neural networks is their ability to learn from their own past activities in the sense that records of the system's past performance can influence processing in order to improve future performance.

Neural simulators Software development programs used to develop neural networks by allowing the developer to specify learning rules that will be used by the individual neurons to adapt their transfer functions.

O

Offensive intelligence An aspect of an organization's strategic intelligence system that seeks to achieve the organization's goals.

On-line data services Vendors that serve as clearinghouses and communications networks for on-line data resources drawn from government, trade associations, and many private data collection agencies.

Open-item system An accounting system in which the firm keeps track of every invoice sent and payments are matched to individual invoices.

Optimization model A type of **analytical model** that aids marketing decision making by helping marketers identify the best values of variables that represent inputs to marketing decisions in order to maximize the achievement of marketing goals.

Order entry The set of procedures by which an order is placed in a form that can be handled by the firm's processing systems.

Organizational procedural controls Written rules and policies established by the organization for maintaining data integrity and system security and for coordinating usage of the system.

Outbound logistics The physical and procedural systems for warehousing goods and transporting them to customers.

P

Passive intelligence An aspect of an organization's strategic intelligence system that yields benchmark data on competitors and other environmental forces.

Phased conversion A type of **phased implementation** in which one MKIS system is gradually replaced by another.

Phased implementation The process of developing the MKIS components as modules and implementing the new MKIS in phases. In this way, the organization can benefit from each component of the MKIS as it becomes available rather than waiting until all components are developed.

Planning The first stage in the MKIS creation process. Planning has the goal of either (1) establishing the environment and guidelines for effective development and implementation of a MKIS or (2) abandoning the MKIS creation effort at an early stage if it is found not to be feasible in light of the organization's resources and priorities.

Point-to-point communications Communications links between each workstation and each CPU on which MKIS data or applications are located.

Political environment Government and legal forces that influence business, including legislation, regulatory agencies, judicial rulings, the threat of legal action, international treaties, tariffs, trade quotas, and even the risk of revolution or changing political parties and leaders.

Private data vendors Nongovernment agencies that provide marketing-related environmental data.

Prospect A **lead** worthy of contact.

Prototyping The process of creating a preliminary model of an anticipated MKIS system so that it can be presented to users for evaluation.

Purchasing and accounts payable systems The formal procedures for making purchasing decisions, verifying that the proper goods or services have been received, and making payment for those goods or services.

Q

Quotation preparation An offer to deliver a specified product or service to a customer, at a specified price, location, and time.

Quote A promise to deliver a good or service by a stated time for a stated price.

R

Raw materials and parts inventory system A system used by the production department to ensure that all materials will be on hand to meet production schedules required by marketing's sales forecasts.

Receiving system A system of procedures by which an organization accepts a shipment of goods or a service and verifies compliance with contract specifications related to the designs of the goods or services and their quality.

Relational database An organized set of data in which the various types of data items from several data sets are sufficiently identified by a predetermined set of criteria so that items may be linked together in a logical way.

Reporting and inquiry system A type of **decision support system** that provides the marketing manager with the ability to inspect company records regarding what has occurred.

Rule editor A specialized text editor used to efficiently enter rules, preconditions, and actions into shell programs for developing expert systems.

Rule interpreter A computer program that executes an expert system shell program, searching for rules that can be executed only when the precondition is true and executing them according to one of several possible priority orders.

S

Safety stock The minimum amount of a specific part that is to be held in inventory before a new order is issued to replenish the inventory.

Sales commission records Data on the payments earned by salespeople as a result of specific sales.

Simulation model A type of **analytical model** that allows explicit consideration of decisions that have *probabilistic*, rather than certain, outcomes. This type of model explicitly recognizes the uncertainty of marketing environments and considers this uncertainty by building probability fluctuations into the predicted outcomes.

Single-source data services Companies that track individual customers' purchases and link this information to store data, product promotion data, neighborhood data, and other socioeconomic data that describe the consumer and the purchaser.

Social environment The cultural and demographic characteristics and trends of the markets in which an organization might participate.

Software requirements The specific decision support software that will provide marketing managers with the analytical and reporting capabilities described in the macrospecifications document.

Software systems controls Administrative capabilities—provided by the operating system software, the communication system software, or specific applications software—that allow a system programmer to create new accounts for persons wishing to use the system, define privileges for each account on the system, set system priorities for accounts and types of activities, and otherwise govern access to system resources.

Standardized workstations Desktop computer systems configured in the same way for all users.

Sustainable competitive advantage An ability or resource that allows the organization to provide an offer to the market that is more acceptable to potential customers than competitors' offers and to maintain this preferred position over a long period.

System administrator A member of the MKIS technical support staff who has access to an account that has the highest level of privileges and who can set privileges for all other accounts.

Systems controls Enforceable rules designed to protect data integrity and security, govern access to the system, and coordinate users' activities.

T

Task-oriented documentation Written instructions designed for the user of the MKIS system and organized around the specific tasks that must be performed.

Technical development The second stage of the MKIS creation process. This is the stage in which actual programming is accomplished and the fundamental system is established.

Technological environment Encompasses a wide range of fields in which new physical innovations and new ways of carrying out activities can affect business operations and market needs or can create new business opportunities.

Testing A step in the MKIS technical development stage in which actual system components are made available to selected marketing managers who then use the system as though it were part of their regular activities so that "real-world" experience may be gained and feedback may be provided to the MKIS team.

U

Unconditional forecast model A type of **forecast model** that predicts future events using historical data but without explicit assumptions about environmental factors.

User interfaces The processes and equipment by which the marketing manager will use the MKIS, including the types of computers that users are willing to use, how information is displayed on paper or on the screen of a terminal or microcomputer, the types of knowledge that may be required to use the system, and the printers and other forms of technology by which reports are produced to document the analysis underlying a decision.

User training A systematic approach to providing users with written documentation, on-line documentation, a help system, and peer support as each component of the MKIS is implemented.

V

Value chain A sequence of activities by which the firm brings "raw materials" into the organization, processes these into finished products that will be desired by the market, and distributes these to customers.

Virus A disruptive computer program planted by someone trying to sabotage a computer system.

Bibliography

Baker, S., and K. Baker (1993). *Market Mapping*. New York: McGraw-Hill.

Barabba, V. P., and G. Zaltman (1992a). "Knowledge Loom of the '90s: An Inquiry Center Uses Technology to Weave Together Marketplace Information for Effective Decision Making." *Computerworld*, Vol. 26, No. 25 (June 22), pp. 133–134.

Barabba, V. P., and G. Zaltman (1992b). "The Right Technical Ingredients: Technologies Such as E-mail, GUIs, Interactive Video Form the Basis of an Inquiry Center." *Computerworld*, Vol. 26, No. 25 (June 22), p. 137.

Baugh, P., A. Gillies, and P. Jastrzebski (1993). "Combining Knowledge-based and Database Technology in a Tool for Business Planning." *Information and Software Technology*, Vol. 35, No. 3 (March), pp. 131–137.

Bedient, J. B. (1989). *Marketing Decision Making Using Lotus 1-2-3*. Cincinnati, OH: Southwestern.

Bennett, P. B. (Ed.). (1988). *Dictionary of Marketing Terms*. Chicago: American Marketing Association.

Berenson, C. (1985). "Marketing Information Systems," *Journal of Marketing*, Vol. 33 (October), pp. 16–23.

Bessen, J. (1993). "Riding the Marketing Information Wave." *Harvard Business Review*, Vol. 71, No. 5 (September–October), pp. 150–160.

Birks, D. F., and J. M. Southan (1990). "The Potential of Marketing Information Systems in Charitable Organisations." *Marketing Intelligence and Planning*, Vol. 8, No. 4, pp. 15–20.

Blattberg, R. C., and R. Glazer (1994). "Marketing in the Information Revolution." In R. C. Blattberg, R. Glazer, and J. D. C. Little (Eds.), *The Marketing Information Revolution*. Boston: Harvard Business School Press.

Blattberg, R. C., R. Glazer, and J. D. C. Little, (Eds.). (1994). *The Marketing Information Revolution*. Boston: Harvard Business School Press.

Bloom, P. N., R. Adler, and G. R. Milne (1994). "Identifying the Legal and Ethical Risks and Costs of Using New Information Technologies to Support Marketing Programs." In R. C. Blattberg, R. Glazer, and J. D. C. Little (Eds.), *The Marketing Information Revolution*. Boston: Harvard Business School Press.

Bonczek, R. H., C. W. Holsapple, and A. B. Whinston (1981). *Foundations of Decision Support Systems*. New York: Academic Press.

Boone, L. E., and D. L. Kurtz (1993). *Contemporary Marketing* (8th ed.). Chicago: Dryden.

Borch, O. J., and G. Hartvigsen (1991). "Knowledge-based Systems for Strategic Market Planning in Small Firms." *Decision Support Systems*, Vol. 7, pp. 145–157.

Bowen, C. (1994). *Compuserve from A to Z*. New York: Random House.

Boynton, A. C., and R. W. Zmud (1984). "An Assessment of Critical Success Factors." *Sloan Management Review* (Summer), pp. 17–27.

Bradley, S. P., J. A. Hausman, and R. L. Nolan (1993). *Globalization, Technology, and Competition: The Fusion of Computers and Telecommunications in the 1990s*. Boston: Harvard University Press.

Bryan, N. S. (1993). "What Are 'Business Geographics' Anyway?" *Business Geographics*, Vol. 1, No. 1 (January/February), pp. 24–25.

Burke, R. R. (1994). "Artificial Intelligence for Designing Marketing Decision-making Tools." In R. C. Blattberg, R. Glazer, and J. D. C. Little (Eds.), *The Marketing Information Revolution*. Boston: Harvard Business School Press.

Burkhart, K. (1993). "Geographic Analysis Ensures Customer Satisfaction." *Business Geographics*, Vol. 1, No. 1 (January/February), pp. 26–27.

Business Week (1994). "Database Marketing." *Business Week*, No. 3388 (September 5), pp. 56–62.

Buttery, E. A., and E.M. Buttery (1991). "Design of Marketing Information Systems: Useful Paradigms." *European Journal of Marketing*, Vol. 25, No. 1, pp. 26–39.

Buzzell, R. D., D. F. Cox, and R. V. Brown (1969). *Market Research and Information Systems*. New York: McGraw-Hill.

Bylinsky, G. (1993). "The Payoff from 3-D Computing." *Fortune*, Vol. 128, No. 7 (Autumn), Special Issue, pp. 32–40.

Campbell, T., V. Duperret-Tran, and T. Campbell II (1994). "Ideal International Accounting Systems: Integrative, Instantaneous, Intelligent, and Intense," In P. C. Deans and K. R. Karwan (Eds.), *Global Information Systems and Technology* (pp. 242–260) Harrisburg, PA: Idea Group.

Caminiti, S. (1993). "A Star Is Born," *Fortune*, Vol. 128, No. 13 (Autumn–Winter), pp. 44–47.

Carroll, J. A. (1992). "Online Intelligence." *CA Magazine*, Vol. 125, No. 8 (August), pp. 26–31.

Cash, J. I., R. G. Eccles, N. Nohria, and R. L. Nolan (1993). *Building the Information Age Organization: Structure, Control, and Information Technologies*. Homewood. IL: Irwin.

Cash, J. I., and B. R. Konsynski (1985). "IS Redraws Competitive Boundaries." *Harvard Business Review*, Vol. 63, No. 2 (March–April), pp. 134–142.

Cash, J. I., F. W. McFarlan, J. L. McKenney, and L. M. Applegate (1992). *Corporate Information Systems Management: Text and Cases*. Homewood, IL: Irwin.

Chadha, S., L. Mazlack, and R. A. Pick (1991). "Using Existing Knowledge Sources (Cases) to Build an Expert System." *Expert Systems: The International Journal of Knowledge Engineering*, Vol. 8 (February), pp. 3–12.

Chandler, J. S., and T. P. Liang (1990). *Developing Expert Systems for Business Applications*. Columbus, OH: Merrill.

Chang, H., and J. Jiang (1993a). "Neural Network Models as an Alternative to Time-Series Forecasting on Scanner Data." *Delta Business Review*, Vol. 3 (Fall/Winter), pp. 25–30.

Chang, H., and J. Jiang (1993b). "Applying Neural Networks on Scanner Data," In D. F. Rogers and A. S. Raturi (Eds.), *Proceedings of the 1993 Annual Meeting of the Decision Sciences Institute* (pp. 598–600). Washington, DC: Decision Sciences Institute (November).

Churchill, G. A., Jr. (1991). *Marketing Research Methedological Foundations*, (5th ed.). Chicago: Dryden.

Clancy, K. J., and R. S. Shulman (1992). "It's Better to Fly a New Product Simulator than to Crash the Real Thing." *Planning Review*, Vol. 20, No. 4 (July/August), pp. 10–17.

Collins, R. H. (1985). "Enhancing Spreadsheets for Increased Productivity." *Journal of Personal Selling and Sales Management*, Vol. 5, No. 2 (November), pp. 79–81.

Cooke, D. F. (1993). "Unlock Your Company's Databases." *Business Geographics*, Vol. 1, No. 1 (January/February), pp. 9–10.

Cox, D. F., and R. E. Goode (1967). "How to Build a Marketing Information System." *Harvard Business Review*, Vol. 45, No. 3, pp. 145–154.

Curry, D. J. (1993). *The New Marketing Research Systems*. New York: Wiley.

Daft, R. L., and R. H. Lengel (1986). "Organizational Information Requirements, Media Richness, and Structural Design." *Management Science*, Vol. 32. (May), pp. 554–571.

Daft, R. L., and K. E. Weick (1984). "Toward a Model of Organizations as Interpretation Systems." *Academy of Management Review*, Vol. 9, No. 2, pp. 284–295.

Darian, J. C. (1989). "Estimating Market and Sales Potential Using a Dialog Data Base," In R. F. Dyer and M. S. Steinberg (Eds.), *Proceedings of the 1989 AMA Microcomputers in the Marketing Curriculum Conference* (pp. 74–82). Chicago: American Marketing Association.

Datapro Reports (1989). *Marketing Information Systems*. New York: McGraw-Hill.

Davis, G. B., and M. H. Olson (1985). *Management Information Systems: Conceptual Foundations, Structure, and Development*. New York: McGraw-Hill.

Davis, K. (1992). "Dear Reader: How They Got Your Name." *Kiplinger's Personal Finance Magazine* (April), pp. 44–47.

Deans, C. P., and M. J. Kane (1992). *International Dimensions of Information Systems and Technology*. Boston: PWS-Kent.

Dialog Information Services, Inc. (1993). *Dialog Database Catalog, 1991*. Palo Alto, CA: Dialog Information Services, Inc.

Dobrozdravic, N. (1989). "Computerized Lead-tracking Analysis Makes Direct Marketing More Effective." *Marketing News*, Vol. 23, No. 11, pp. 27–28.

Dunne, P. M., and H. I. Wolk (1977). "Marketing Cost Analysis: A Modularized Contribution Approach" *Journal of Marketing* (July), pp. 83–94.

Dyer, R. F., and E. H. Forman (1991). *An Analytic Approach to Marketing Decisions*. Englewood Cliffs, NJ: Prentice Hall.

Eisenhart, T. (1988). "Computer Aided Marketing." *Business Marketing*, Vol. 73, No. 5 (May), pp. 49–56.

Eisenhart, T. (1990). "After 10 Years of Marketing Decision Support Systems, Where's the Payoff?" *Business Marketing* (June), pp. 46-51.

Fletcher, K., and A. Buttery (1988). "The Structure and Content of the Marketing Information System: A Guide for Management." *Marketing Intelligence and Planning*, Vol. 6, No. 4, pp. 27–35.

Fortune (1993a). "How to Bolster the Bottom Line." *Fortune*, Vol. 128, No. 7 (Autumn), Special Issue, pp. 14–28.

Fortune (1993b). "Making It All Worker-Friendly." *Fortune*, Vol. 128, No. 7 (Autumn), Special Issue, pp. 44–53.

Fortune (1993c). "Meet the New Consumer." *Fortune*, Vol. 128, No. 13 (Autumn/Winter), Special Issue, pp. 6–7.

Francica, J. R. (1993). "Improve Your Market Expansion Planning by Integrating Geography." *Business Geographics*, Vol. 1, No. 1 (January/February), pp. 13–14.

Gallagher, J. P. (1988). *Knowledge Systems for Business: Integrating Expert Systems and MIS*. Englewood Cliffs, NJ: Prentice Hall.

Gendelev, B. (1992). "MIS and Marketing: Secrets of Strategic Information Mining." *Chief Information Officer Journal*, Vol. 5, No. 1 (Summer), pp. 12–16.

Gilbert, S. (1992). "Information Management: A Mountain Climber's Guide," *Sales and Marketing Management*, Vol. 144, No. 8 (July), pp. 97–101.

GIS NewsLink (1993). "GIS Used for Loan Discrimination Study." *GIS World*, Vol. 6, No. 10 (October), p. 9.

Glazer, R. (1991). "Marketing in an Information-intensive Environment: Strategic Implications of Knowledge as an Asset" *Journal of Marketing*, Vol. 55, No. 4 (October), pp. 1–9.

Gray, J., and A. Reuter (1993). *Transaction Processing: Concepts and Techniques*. San Mateo, CA: Morgan Kaufmann.

Gray, P. (1988). *Guide to IFPS/Personal*. New York: McGraw-Hill.

Gray, P., and P. Olfman (1989). "The User Interface in Group Decision Support Systems." *Decision Support Systems*, Vol. 5, (June), pp. 119–138.

Greco, A. J., and J. T. Hogue (1990). "Developing Marketing Decision Support Systems." *Journal of Business and Industrial Marketing*, Vol. 5, No. 2 (Summer/Fall), pp. 27–36.

Green, P. E. (1992). "Paradigms, Paradiddles, and Parafoils." *Journal of the Academy of Marketing Science*, Vol. 20, No. 4 (Fall), pp. 377–378.

Green, P. E., and A. M. Krieger (1992). "An Application of a Product Positioning Model to Pharmaceutical Products." *Marketing Science*, Vol. 11, No. 2 (Spring), 117–132.

Guadagni, P. M., and J. D. C. Little (1983). "A Logit Model of Brand Choice Calibrated on Scanner Data." *Marketing Science*, Vol. 2, No. 3 (Summer), pp. 203–238.

Hackman, R. J., and G. R. Oldham (1980). *Work Redesign*. Reading, MA: Addison-Wesley.

Hall, L. D., and K. P. Marshall (1992). *Computing for Social Research: Practical Approaches*. Belmont, CA: Wadsworth.

Hambrick, D. C. (1982). "Environmental Scanning and Organizational Strategy," Strategic *Management Journal*, Vol. 3, pp. 159–174.

Harvard Business School (1982). *Information Resources, Inc. (A)*. (Case 9-583-053 Rev. 11/84). Boston: Harvard Business School.

Harvard Business School (1983). *Information Resources, Inc. (B)*. (Case 9-584-044 Rev. 7/84). Boston: Harvard Business School.

Higby, M. A., and B. N. Farah. (1991). "The Status of Marketing Information Systems, Decision Support Systems, and Expert Systems in the Marketing Function of U.S. Firms." *Information and Management*, Vol. 20, No. 1 (January), pp. 29-35.

Hoch, S. J. (1994). "Experts and Models in Combination." In R. C. Blattberg, R. Glazer, and J. D. C. Little (Eds.), *The Marketing Information Revolution*. Boston: Harvard Business School Press.

Holsapple, C. W., and A. B. Whinston (1987). *Business Expert Systems*. Homewood, IL: Irwin.

Ing, D. (1994). "The Evolution of Decision Support Systems and Databases in Consumer Goods Marketing," In R. C. Blattberg, R. Glazer, and J. D. C. Little (Eds.), The Marketing Information Revolution. Boston: Harvard Business School Press.

Ingram, B., (1992). "Market Metrics' Quest to Sell Micro-marketing," *Supermarket Business*, Vol. 47, No. 10 (October), pp. 27–32.

Ives, B., and M. H. Olson, (1984). "User Involvement and MIS Success: A Review of Research." *Management Science*, Vol. 30, No. 5. (May), pp. 586–603.

Jiang, J. J., D. J. Curry, and R. A. Pick (1993). "User Assistance in Model-based Decision Support Systems." In D. F. Rogers and A. S. Raturi (Eds). *Proceedings of the 1993 Annual Meeting of the Decision Sciences Institute* (pp. 675–677). Washington, DC: Decision Sciences Institute (November).

Johnson, C. M. (1989). "On-line Corporate Intelligence in Marketing Research Courses" In R. F. Dyer and M. S. Steinberg (Eds.), *Proceedings of the 1989 AMA Microcomputers in the Marketing Curriculum Conference*, (pp. 66–73). Chicago: American Marketing Association,.

Kane, P. (1991). *Prodigy Made Easy*. Berkeley, CA: Osborne-McGraw.

Keen, P. G. (1981). "Information Systems and Organizational Change." *Communications of the Association for Computing Machinery (ACM)*, Vol. 24, No. 1, pp. 24–33.

Keon, E. F. (1987). "Making MKIS Work for You." *Business Marketing*, Vol. 72, No. 10, pp. 71–73.

Kestelyn, J. (1992). "Application Watch." *AI Expert* (January), pp. 63–64.

Kotler, P. (1991). *Marketing Management: Analysis, Planning, Implementation, and Control*. (7th ed.). Englewood Cliffs, NJ: Prentice Hall.

Kotler, P., and A. Andreasen (1991). *Strategic Marketing for Nonprofit Organizations*. Englewood Cliffs, NJ: Prentice Hall.

Kotler, P., W. Gregor, and W. Rogers (1977). "The Marketing Audit Comes of Age." *Sloan Management Review* (Winter), pp. 25–43.

Krcmar, H. A. O., and H. C. Lucas, Jr. (1991). "Success Factors for Strategic Information Systems." *Information and Management*, Vol. 21, No. 3 (October), pp. 137–145.

Krol, E. (1992). *The Whole Internet User's Guide and Catalog*. Sebastopol, CA: O'Reilly and Associates.

Larreche, J. C., and V. Srinivasan (1981). "Stratport: A Decision Support System for Strategic Planning." *Journal of Marketing*, (Fall), pp. 39–52.

Laudon, K. C., and P. P. Laudon (1988). *Management Information Systems: A Contemporary Perspective*. New York: Macmillan.

Lea, A., and P. Direzze (1993). "The More Functionality, the Better the Retail Analysis." *Business Geographics*, Vol. 1, No. 1 (January/February), pp. 33–38.

Leeflang, P. S. H., and D. R. Wittink (1992). "Diagnosing Competitive Reactions Using (Aggregated) Scanner Data." *International Journal of Research in Marketing*, Vol. 9, pp. 39–57.

Lichty, T. (1993). *The Official America Online Tour Guide*. Chapel Hill, NC: Ventana Press.

Liesse, J. (1993). "New IRI Division Targets Trade Promotions." *Advertising Age*, Vol. 64, No. 8 (February 22), p. 43.

Lilien, G. L., P. Kotler, and K. S. Moorthy (1992). *Marketing Models*. Englewood Cliffs, NJ: Prentice Hall.

Little, J. D. C. (1979). "Decision Support Systems for Marketing Managers." *Journal of Marketing*, Vol. 43 (Summer), pp. 9–26.

Little, J. D. C. (1990). "Operations Research in Industry: New Opportunities in a Changing World." *The 1990 Philip McCord Morse Lecture, ORSA/TIMS Joint National Meeting*. Philadelphia: ORSA/Times (October 29).

Littlefield, J. P. (1992). "Pouncing on Perfect Customers." *Canadian Banker*, Vol 99, No. 5 (May/June), pp. 50–51.

Lodish, L. M. (1982). "A Marketing Decision Support System for Retailers." *Marketing Science*, Vol. 1, No. 1 (Winter), pp. 31–56.

Lucas, H. C. (1986). *Information Systems Concepts for Management* (3rd ed.). New York: McGraw-Hill.

McCann, J. M. (1986). *The Marketing Workbench*. Homewood, IL: Dow Jones–Irwin.

McCann, J. M., and J. P. Gallagher (1990). *Expert Systems for Scanner Data Environments: The Marketing Workbench Laboratory Experience*. Boston: Kluwer Academic Publishers.

McCann, J. M., A. Tadlaoui, and J. P. Gallagher (1990). "Knowledge Systems in Merchandising: Advertising Design." *Journal of Retailing* , Vol. 66, (Fall), pp. 257–277.

McCarthy, J. E. (1960). *Basic Marketing*. Homewood, IL: Irwin.

McCarthy, J. E., and W. D. Perreault, Jr. (1993). *Basic Marketing: A Global Managerial Approach*. Homewood, IL: Irwin.

McFadden, F. R., and J. A. Hoffer (1991). *Database Management* (3rd ed.). Redwood City, CA: Benjamin/Cummings.

Malhotra, N. K. (1992). "Shifting Perspective on the Shifting Paradigm in Marketing Research: A New Paradigm in Marketing Research." *Journal of the Academy of Marketing Science*, Vol. 20, No. 4 (Fall), pp. 379–387.

Marshall, K. P. (1994). "Global Perspectives on Marketing Information Systems: Challenges and Opportunities." In C. Deans and K. Karwan (Eds.), *Global Information Systems and Technology: Focus on the Organization and Its Functional Areas* (pp. 33–59). Harrisburg, PA: Idea Group.

Marshall, K. P., and S. W. Lamotte (1992). "Marketing Information Systems: A Marriage of Systems Analysis and Marketing Management." *Journal of Applied Business Research*, Vol. 8, No. 3 (Summer), pp. 61–73.

Mason, R. (1986). "Four Ethical Issues of the Information Age." *MIS Quarterly*, Vol. 10, No. 1 (January), pp. 486–498.

Mayros, V., and D. J. Dolan (1988). "Hefting the Data Load: How to Design the MKIS That Works for You." *Business Marketing* (March), pp. 47–69.

Mayros, V., and D. M. Werner (1982). *Marketing Information Systems: Design and Applications for Marketers*. Radnor, PA: Chilton.

Mentzer, J. T., and N. Gandhi (1992). "Expert Systems in Marketing: Guidelines for Development." *Journal of the Academy of Marketing Sciences*, Vol. 20 (Winter), pp. 71–80.

Metzger, G. D. (1990). "Single Source: Yes and No (the Backward View)." *Marketing Research* (December), pp. 27–33.

Mohan, L., and W. K. Holstein (1994). "Marketing Decision Support Systems in Transition." In R. C. Blattberg, R. Glazer, and J. D. C. Little (Eds.), *The Marketing Information Revolution*. Boston: Harvard Business School Press.

Montgomery, D. B., and C. B. Weinberg (1979). "Toward Strategic Intelligence Systems." *Journal of Marketing*, Vol. 43 (Fall), pp. 41–52.

Moriarty, R. T., and G. S. Swartz (1989). "Automation to Boost Sales and Marketing." *Harvard Business Review*, Vol. 67, No. 1, pp. 100–108.

Muhanna, W. A., and R. A. Pick (1994). "Meta-modeling Concepts and Tools for Model Management: A Systems Approach." *Management Science*, Vol. 40 (September), pp. 1093–1123.

Mumford, E., and M. Weir (1979). *Computer Systems and Work Design: The ETHICS Method*. New York: Wiley.

Nilsson, N. J. (1980). *Principles of Artificial Intelligence*. Palo Alto, CA: Tioga.

Nylen, David W. (1990). *Marketing Decision-making Handbook*. Englewood Cliffs, NJ: Prentice Hall.

O'Brien, T. V. (1990). "Decision Support Systems." *Marketing Research* (December), pp. 51–55.

O'Callaghan, R., P. J. Daufman, and B. R. Konsynski (1992). "Adoption Correlates and Share Effects of Electronic Data Interchange Systems in Marketing Channels." *Journal of Marketing*, Vol. 56, No. 2 (April), pp. 45–56.

Overhultz, G. (1993). "Data Integration Unlocks Valuable Marketing Information." *Marketing News*, Vol. 27, No. 19 (September 13), p. 8.

Pare, T. P. (1993). "How to Find out What They Want." *Fortune*, Vol. 128, No. 13 (Autumn/Winter), pp. 39–41.

Perreault, W. D., Jr. (1992). "The Shifting Paradigm in Marketing Research." *Journal of the Academy of Marketing Science*, Vol. 20, No. 4 (Fall), pp. 367–375.

Peters, B. (1990). "The 'Brave New World' of Single Source Information." *Marketing Research*, (December) pp. 13–21.

Peters, T., and N. Austin (1985). *A Passion for Excellence*. New York: Random House.

Pigford, D., and G. Baur (1995). *Expert Systems for Business: Concepts and Applications,* (2nd ed.). Boston: boyd & fraser.

Pittman, R. H. (1990). Geographic Information Systems: An Important Tool for Economic Development Professionals." *Economic Development Review*, Vol. 8, No. 4 (Fall), pp. 4–7.

Porter, M. E. (1980). *Competitive Strategy: Techniques for Analyzing Industries and Competitors*. New York: Free Press.

Porter, M. E. (1985). *Competitive Advantage: Creating and Sustaining Superior Performance*. New York: Free Press.

Porter, M. E., and V. E. Millar (1985). "How Information Gives You Competitive Advantage." *Harvard Business Review*, Vol. 63, No. 4 (July–August), pp. 149–160.

Pratt, P. J. (1990). *Microcomputer Database Management Using dBASE IV*. Boston: boyd & fraser.

Pride, W. M., and O. C. Ferrell (1993). *Marketing Concepts and Strategies* (8th ed.). Boston: Houghton Mifflin.

Prince, M. (1990). "Some Uses and Abuses of Single Source Data for Promotional Decision Making." *Marketing Research* (December), pp. 18–22.

Proctor, R. A. (1992). "Marketing Decision Support Systems: A Role for Neural Networking." *Marketing Intelligence and Planning*, Vol. 10, No. 1, pp. 21–26.

Proctor, R. A. (1991). "Marketing Information Systems." *Management Decision*, Vol. 29, No. 4, pp. 55–60.

Ramachandran, Kavil (1991). "Data Collection for Management Research in Developing Countries." In N. C. Smith and P. Dainty (Eds.), *The Management Research Handbook*. London: Routledge.

Rice, F. (1993). "New Rules of Superlative Service." *Fortune*, Vol. 128, No. 13 (Autumn/Winter), pp. 50–53.

Robins, G. (1992). "Marketing—Canadian Tire's MIPS Project: Changing the Pipeline." *Stores*, Vol. 74, No. 10 (October), pp. 36–38.

Rochester, J. B. (1992). "Computer/Telephone Integration for Marketing Information Systems." *I/S Analyzer*, Vol. 30 (June), pp. 1–10.

Rothfeder, J. (1992). "Taking a Byte out of Privacy." *USA Weekend*, (August 28–30), pp. 4–6.

Rothfeder, J., J. Bartino, L. Therman, and R. Brandt (1990). "How Software Is Making Food Sales a Piece of Cake: 'Decision Support Systems.," *Business Week*, No. 3167 (July 2), pp. 54–56.

Rubinstein, E. (1989). "Food Manufacturers Discover Value of Intelligence Systems." *Marketing News*, Vol. 23, No. 11, (May 22) p.11

Runnels, D. (1993). "Geographic-based System Rescues Insurers." *Business Geographics*, Vol. 1, No. 1 (January/February) 94, pp. 30–32.

Sales and Marketing Management (1994). *1994 Survey of Buying Power*. (August 7).

SAS Institute (1985). *The SAS System: Your Software Solution*, (Videotapes, Parts 1 and 2). Cary, NC: SAS Institute.

Schmitz, J. (1994). "Expert Systems for Scanner Data in Practice." In R. C. Blattberg, R. Glazer, and J. D. C. Little (Eds.), *The Marketing Information Revolution*. Boston: Harvard Business School Press.

Schmitz, J. D., G. D. Armstrong, and J. D. C. Little (1990). "CoverStory: Automated News Finding in Marketing." *Interfaces*, Vol. 20, No. 6 (November–December), pp. 29–38.

Sellers, P. (1993). "Keeping the Buyers You Have." *Fortune*, Vol. 128, No. 13 (Autumn/Winter), pp. 56–58.

Simon, R. (1992). "Stop Them from Selling Your Financial Secrets." *Money* (March), pp. 99–110.

Singh, M. G., J. C. Bennavail, and Z. J. Chen (1992). "A Group Decision Tool for Combining Subjective Estimates Based on an Optimisation Approach." *Decision Support Systems*, Vol. 8, No. 6 (November), pp. 541–549.

Sisodia, R. S. (1992). "Marketing Information and Decision Support Systems for Services." *Journal of Services Marketing*, Vol. 6, No. 1 (Winter), pp. 51–64.

Steinberg, M., and R. E. Plank (1990). "Implementing Expert Systems into Business-to-Business Marketing Practice." *Journal of Business and Industrial Marketing*, Vol. 5, No. 2 (Summer/Fall), pp. 15–26.

Steinberg, M., and R. E. Plank (1987). "Expert Systems: The Integrative Sales Management Tool of the Future." *Journal of the Academy of Marketing Science*, Vol. 15, No. 2 (Summer), pp. 55–62.

Stewart, D. W. (1984). *Secondary Research: Information Sources and Methods*. Newbury Park, CA: Sage.

Stewart, D. W., and P. N. Shamdasani (1990). *Focus Groups: Theory and Practice*. Newbury Park, CA: Sage.

Tavakoli, A. (1993). "GIS Eases Banking's Regulatory Compliance Efforts." *Business Geographics*, Vol. 1, No. 1 (January/February), p. 22.

Tetzell, R. (1993). "Mapping for Dollars." *Fortune*, Vol. 128, No. 9 (October 18), pp. 91–96.

Tieperman, J., R. A. Inman, and R. A. Pick (1994). "Expert Systems: A Service Industry Exigency." *Industrial Management and Data Systems*, Vol. 94, No. 1, pp. 9–12.

Triste, A. N., and P. R. Lawrence (1963). *Organizational Choice*. London: Travistock.

U.S. Bureau of the Census (1993). *Census Catalogue and Guide: 1993*. Washington, DC: U.S. Department of Commerce.

U.S. Bureau of the Census (1989). *County Business Patterns*. Washington, DC: U.S. Department of Commerce.

Westland, J. C. (1992). "Self-organizing Executive Information Networks." *Decision Support Systems*, Vol. 8, pp. 41–53.

Wheelwright, S. C., and S. Makridakis (1985). *Forecasting Methods for Management* (4th ed.). New York: Wiley.

Williams, R. J. (1966). "Marketing Intelligence Systems: A DEW Line for Marketing Men." *Business Management* (January), p. 32.

Winters, L. C. (1990). "Micro-targeting." *Marketing Research* (September), pp. 62–64.

Wiseman, C. (1988). *Strategic Information Systems*. Homewood, IL: Irwin.

Wiseman, C. (1985). *Strategy and Computers*. Homewood, IL: Dow Jones–Irwin.

Wolfe, M. J. (1990). " '90s Will See 'Great Leap Forward' in Sales Tracking." *Marketing News*, Vol. 24, No. 18 (September 3), pp. 2, 5.

Woodward, J. (1965). *Industrial Organization: Theory and Practice*. London: Oxford University Press.

Zahedi, F. (1993). *Intelligent Systems for Business: Expert Systems with Neural Networks*. Belmont, CA: Wadsworth.

Zikmund, W. G., and M. d'Amico (1993). *Marketing*. Eagan, MN: West.

Subject Index

macrospecifications, 90, 94–96
manufacturing, 129, 130
market segments, 35, 38, 62
marketing
  4Ps of, 13
  definition of, 3
  scope of, 12–14
  trends in, 128–130
  See also advertising, promotions
marketing audit, 90–92, 122
marketing functions audit, 96
"Marketing in the Information Revolution", 129
marketing department
  activities, 12–14, 16, 83
  director, 14, 89, 90
  information requirements, 14–17
  MKIS creation, 88, 89–90, 112
  product manager, 14, 15, 18, 31, 57, 60, 93
  research, 13, 14, 35, 49–50, 126–127
  role in organization, 12
  See also advertising, promotions
marketing information system (MKIS)
  consultants, 90, 106, 110
  creation process, 83–86
  description of, 3–5, 12
  future trends, 128
  vision of, 88–89, 96
  See also implementation, planning, technical development
marketing intelligence system, 49–50
marketing mix, 13, 49
Marketing News, 106
marketing organization audit, 91–92
marketing productivity audit, 92
marketing strategies audit, 91
marketing systems audit, 92
Martin, Tom, 36
media outlets, selecting, 15
micromarketing, 129
MicroScan, 37
MIT, 72
mixed distributed processing system, 106–107, 109
MKIS. See marketing information system (MKIS)
models. See analytical models
modular component analysis, 59–60, 140
multicriteria model, 64

National Decisions Systems, 48
NBI, 21
neural networks, 75–78
Nielsen, A. C., 47, 49
North American Free Trade Agreement (NAFTA), 23
Novell's baseband Ethernet, 109

Ocean Spray Cranberries, 72, 128
offensive intelligence, 19–20
on-line data services, 48
open-item system, 39
operations, 18, 32
optimization model, 63–64
order entry, 37–38
organizational goals, 90, 93–94
organizational procedural controls, 110
outbound logistics, 18, 32–34

Paradox database management system, 141
passive intelligence, 19
PepsiCo, 61
PerView networking software, 39
phased implementation, 86, 118–119
planning, 85, 86
  budgeting, 96
  end-user programming, 83
  executive commitment, 87–89, 94, 121, 123
  macrospecifications, 94–96
  marketing audit, 90–92
  MKIS team, 89–90
  organizational goals, 90, 92–94
Philip Morris, 35
point-of-sale (POS) computer systems, 45
point-to-point communications, 108–109
political environment, 23
potential markets, identifying, 12–13
Price Analysis System (PAS), 64
pricing, 13, 15, 18, 20–21, 130
printers, 107, 108
private data vendors, 47, 48
procedures, MKIS, 110–111
Prodigy, 48
product manager, 14, 15, 18, 31, 57, 60, 93
production operations, 18, 32
profitability, maximizing, 64
programming shell, 74–75
promotions
  assessing impact of, 45, 62
  planning, 32, 35
  selecting tactics for, 72
proposals, 36
prospects, 35–36
prototypes, 85, 112–113
purchasing and accounts payable systems, 30–31
purchasing and retail support, 62

Quattro Pro for Windows, 64
quotation systems, 36–37

raw materials and parts inventory system, 31–32
receiving system, 31
record format, 136–137
relational databases, 7, 19, 102–103, 139–141
reporting and inquiry systems, 57, 65
  exception reports, 58–59
  geographic mapping, 60–61
  graphical displays, 60
  user-designed reports, 58
resources, MKIS, 108, 118–119
retailers, 44–45, 129
risk assessment, 63
rule editor, 75
rule interpreter, 75

safety stock, 31–32, 45
sales
  distinguishing problems with, 15
  forecasting, 62, 72, 77
  monitoring, 18–19, 22
  setting quotas, 15–16, 69, 72
  set sales quotas, 69, 72

Author Index